Biblical

"1 Page Briefs"

VOLUME 2

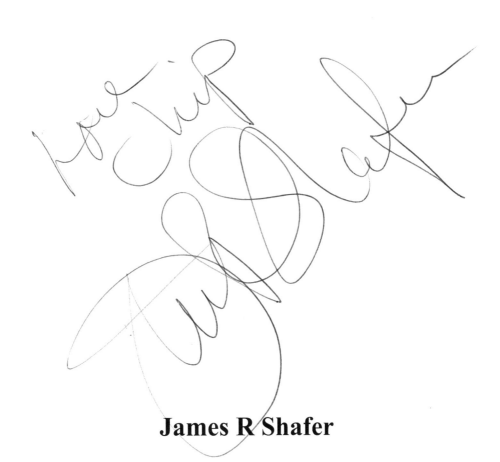

James R Shafer

Dedication

In working backward, I now want to stop and thank my children. One went to Jesus three days after birth. That was John. Our second was Suzette, and our third was Peter. No family is perfect or protected. Suzie was the perfect daughter who gave us great joy and fulfilled every desire for a parent. She took charge from the beginning, did well in school, finished college, and married our fine, hardworking son-in-law Steve. The key thing is that he played golf. ☺

Suzie asked Jesus to forgive her, and enter her life in grade school. She asked to be baptized in our friend's pool shortly thereafter. Steve and Suzie gave us the pleasure of their wedding in Aspen, Colorado. Then they gave us the joy of our 3 grandchildren to whom I dedicated my first volume. Any grandparent would appreciate that. The family experiences, trips, and celebrations were memorable.

Next we were given Pete. He followed the lead of the prodigal son in Jesus' parable. In fairness, Pete greatly enhanced my prayer life; especially through the teens and 20's. Pete came back to Jesus in his forties when the grandchildren visited, and he was baptized with them witnessing. Pete has been a hard worker in the second half, and his growing faith has helped and enriched our family experience as did the prodigal son in The Scripture (Luke 15: 11-32).

I can speak to a grand life trip for me. But assuredly, it was, in the main, due to the family with which God graced me!

Acknowledgement

About the Author

It all began in Rutherford New Jersey 80 years ago. After that, it was Battle Creek, Mi., Kansas, California, Denver, and Arizona. After 4 average college years, learning the most out of championship football, I spent another year of post graduate work looking at A's and B's. A struggled career ended up with a National Sales position, and the management. Which I enjoyed.

Instead of accepting Law school in Chicago, I chose marriage, and spent the years studying the Bible. At long last I wished to share that, and thus my "1 Page Briefs" is here. My hope is to get readers introduced to God's Word without having to over read topics.

I think the sales career taught me to keep it simple, and get the order. My motivation was to share with my grandkids what I have learned over the years.

I am obviously not a scholar, but that is my advantage. My business success and failures have honed my skills and given me focus in life. I am just one man passing through. But maybe I will give someone a few good ideas for the trip; especially my grandkids!

About the Book

In this second volume of my "Briefs", I continue, in Spirit, to write on topics that lead to The Scripture. I am attempting to stay away from opinions, and stick to the concept: Get into the Bible!

You will and can learn all about life.

Creation: "In the beginning God created the heavens and the earth" (Genesis 1: 1).

Watching Over us: "It is He who sits above the circle of the earth" (Isaiah 40: 22).

Finally: "I am the Alpha and the Omega, says the Lord God, Who is and Who was and Who is to come, the Almighty" (Revelation 1: 8). That covers it folks, the entire clock of existence.

"Therefore do not be anxious for tomorrow; for tomorrow will care for itself!" (Matthew 6: 34).

I find this volume set a bit more interesting than the first. We will touch on some Theology (the study of God), some topics focused on the Bible's statement concerning the End of Time, of the current story line (some call a dispensation), the Book of Daniel in one pagers, and even God ordained Climate change. The goal is to help the "new born" get into the Bible, being led in by topics of curiosity. I have learned over 5 decades that no other book is more historical, more scientific, or more verified, then the 66 books of The Scripture.

Maybe that is why the Bible has become the "WORLD'S BEST SELLING BOOK" since the printing press was invented!

Table of Contents

The Battlefield #1

This "Brief" is a part of a triage that I have written in response to the past weeks' sermons and a three-day seminar on Theology. It is basically an overview on Theology verses Politics. Theology is the study of God. Politics is basically the government of people. I use, and always will refer to the Holy Bible for my God-perspective. I use the Declaration of Independence and the US Constitution for my political perspective. I am an American Christian, and I enjoy my salvation and freedom!

Pastor Jon covered the perspective of Christianity as he taught us from the Bible text covered in the Book of John 3. Mike and James created their conjoined seminar on theology of Marxism. I have done my "best" to relay my thoughts on these topics in two other "Briefs" in this volume. The basic summation is that you are either God-fearing or Godless. I praise God that I am God-Fearing (Ephesians 2: 8, 9).

The second evaluation deals with the attacks on the first. Godless ideologies are created, very simply to attack the veracity of God's The Scriptures. They are utilized in politics. One might conclude its God or Government.

The messages from Jon were strictly Scriptural, exegetes, and as always, educational. The value of Jon's methodology is enormous as one slowly, but surely, paces through verses, and slows long enough to see what might normally be passed/glossed over in normal reading. This focus in John 3: 31-36 is that it quoted Christ as having come "from above". Our figure of worship was not created out of dust like me, or Mohammad, or Buddha, or Hindu! He was/is, the Creator!

So why are there all these attacks? In Marxism, attacking is a constant. Kant set up the system that two attacking theses' will battle until they reach a settlement referred to as Synthesis. They cannot sit still as the new synthesis, and that is why it moves on to the next theses to battle on in the process. The common enemy of this process then in politics is Faith in our Creator.

Socialism comes from the dust and evolves as it moves up the political spectrum toward Nirvana (Which it can never reach). Along the way it slows down, as a few powerful leaders stall the latest set of lies for power, praise, and possessions.

Freedom and Capitalism (with Christianity) seeks to reach a commonwealth where the individual is the focus. In Statehood, where individual states are the focus! In Nationalism where the Nation operates to the benefit of the collective peoples in a servant role. It is a constant battle from both, inside and outside, to maintain that program and sets of laws.

What an amazing two weeks. The God-perspective and the man-perspective! I trust you will enjoy the other briefs and be educated. In the year of this writing we have a country to save. I believe that this is our role. In the parlance of physical salvation we must need to be praying to God, our Creator and Sustainer that He may save our land. As I also write at this time, my area of topography is drying up. Drought? Only prayer can stop that. The World is also engulfed in wars; hither, thither, and yon! Are you ready?

Be A Part Of The Solution!

See "Christ From Above" and "God-fearing verse Godless"

God-Fearing Versus Godless #2

In the first volume of Biblical Briefs, I wrote on the above title to delineate between those who did believe and those who did not. As I return to the political spectrum again, I am bouncing off reaction to a conference at my church on theology of Marxism. In the Hegelian political process, our lecturer shared the concept that led to man's improved status, or politics, or societies, to a synthesis likened to things getting better.

Do not laugh! Nebuchadnezzar did it in Daniel chapter 3 when he had a monumental statue built for him. It was pure gold; ninety feet high and nine feet wide. That is a lot of gold folks, even in those days. He then required everyone to bow down and worship his idol which Daniels associates did not do. The punishment for that was to be thrown into a fiery furnace. For the final result you can read the rest of chapter 3 later.

My point is that in the name of power politics, anything goes. There seems, however, to be a major split in motivation. We see today that politicians wish to require obedience even in a free country like the USA. Can you spell pandemic? People recently wore masks, closed their churches, stayed 6 ft. apart, and stayed home for work. In Daniel's day you were cooked. Today you were fined, closed down, or turned away from the travel gate.

Those who are Godless took over. These leaders implemented requirements which usurped constitutional rights. Their thinking process is based on power, praise, or possessions, was activated. As our lecturers conveyed, the leaders activated to a higher synthesis. Thesis was freedom. The antithesis was public safety. The synthesis was punishment and control. Christians in general, and certainly in particular, took umbrage to the social enactments.

The "why" of a Christian's reaction to nationally appointed doctors, is a firm belief in the Creator of the world and the founders of our country! This country was the first in history that was founded by men of faith, seeking to exercise their Godly faith. There is no synthesis when it comes to God. He is the Trinitarian Deity who is Omnipotent, Omniscient, and Omnipresent. Those of us saved from our rule-breaking sins, listed ten times in Exodus 20, have asked for forgiveness from our Creator. We see God involved in our life and liberty, in each and every corner of existence.

Our lecturers educated us on the man-developed means for improvement. As usual, every man-created system has major flaws. Therefore, when one has a thesis, which is countered by its antitheses, the so-called improved synthesis is still a man-conceived play-on-life, liberty, and the pursuit of happiness. It always has, and always will corrupt and fail.

Therefore, one can conclude:

One Fears His Creator, Or One Is Godless!

Christ From Above #3

Pastor Jon has been leading us through the greatest salvation chapter in the Scripture this past month or two; John 3. The world we live in has heard about John 3: 16, even at sporting events! But the last couple of weeks, he has focused on verses 31-36. This is where Christ testifies to being "from above". He compares that to others being "from the earth".

He refers to Himself as having been "He whom God has sent". Later on in John 8: 23, He states, "you are from below, I am from above". Now using these up and down words might be glossed over in quick perusal. But if one stops to ponder, Christ is making a distinction. What does He mean other than that He is from another dimension than earth? I gave this some thought and considered how many dimensions we see today, from the microscopic to the universal. Size is relevant!

When one looks through an electron microscope, small bacterium can be seen with little propellers moving them around. With a telescope, gigantic stars appear as twinkles. From box seats at Madison Square Garden, I thought seven feet basketball players looked like midgets. Are you getting the picture? Is it possible our giant universe exists in a box? From what we have seen, from fantasy to films, there is the possibility for all types of perspectives. Especially in size!

We do see however, where we came from in Genesis 2: 7: "the Lord God formed man of dust from the ground" Do you get it? The Bible says that we were created out of dust. It makes perfect sense that Darwin in his non-belief would make up our evolving from something already in existence, because he could not imagine making us out of nothing, or at best; dirt. It is in the Scripture, and I believe it! It then makes sense that Christ would distinguish Himself as having come from above.

I look forward to going up to heaven, just as Paul did (2 Corinthians 12: 2), and just like Christ did in Acts 1: 9: "He was lifted up". Remember in Luke 2: 13, when a "multitude" of angels showed up for

Christ's birth? Back toward the beginning, Enoch was "taken" alive, and later Elijah was taken off "in a whirlwind" (2 Kings 2: 11). I realize/believe these examples were written down to show believers that are led to these The Scriptures, that a future in the heaven is assured! Why else would these examples be in The Scripture unless they were real?

So while believers in their Creator, work out their salvation; having been given and guaranteed the same (Ephesians 2: 8, 9), and aim for the perfected truth (Jesus Christ) (John 14: 6), the "evolved" members of society are busy synthesizing their arguments, wars, disagreement, hypotheses, etc., hoping to synthesize themselves into a better existence as they observe the luckier leaders rule themselves into untold riches and power. At least that has been the history.

I encourage you my (young) friend, "repent and be baptized" (Acts 2: 38), "for the forgiveness of your sins" (breaking God's good laws including loving your neighbor). In this process you will no longer need to synthesize. You are reaching out to your Creator. As the earthly ones attempt to improve on life without God (Socialism), we can attempt self-improvement and love toward our fellow man. It is worth the try, and I will tell you personally that:

It works!

Three Beautiful Women #4

I watched a musical about Esther the other night, and it made me think of just how beautiful a woman could be in submission and attitude. I am sure there are many more, but three came to mind in the present. Beautiful women have always been beautiful, and yet with minor or forgiven flaws. Take Eve, the Biblical mother of civilization, who was tempted. Take Sarah who laughed at God's announcement. Take Lot's wife who looked back and was "salted". Take Bathsheba who committed adultery with David and later birthed the wisest and richest man in history. Take Mary Magdalene who was a reborn prostitute. These were now beautiful, based on imputed righteousness or salvation if you will.

But the story of Esther made me think of a female super-class. The three I thought of were Esther, Ruth, and of course Mary, the one God picked to be the human physical mother of Jesus. These three women were set apart as beautiful women of attitude. That is right; attitude! They had great attitudes of submission, helps, and service.

Ruth and Esther had Bible books written about them. Ruth got married, lost her husband, followed her mother-in-law back to Israel, married Boaz after working his fields, and became David's great grandmother. What a lovely, submissive, loyal woman. She was included in Christ's lineage.

Esther was another kindred spirit. She was not only a lovely woman, she was the lovely woman. Do you know what I mean? So the current queen had an attitude problem, and the King dumped her. Esther's cousin was raising her as she was orphaned. He presented her for the Kings Beauty contest. She became Miss Universe in Persia, and was used by God to save the Jews of her day from the anti-Semites in power. She was not a conniving aggressive feminist, but rather a humble, beautiful, woman, who the King fell in love with and made her Queen.

Lastly, I submit Mary. This beautiful teenaged virgin, was picked by God to be the human mother impregnated by the Holy Spirit. If it were not a historic fact, it would sound like a Greek-god story. She was beautiful and gracious in all that we read about her. She followed Christ from the manger to the cross. She wept tears of joy, and tears of sorrow. I adore that woman for her role in my Saviors life, but I do not worship her. Jesus rebuked a woman giving blessing to Mary for Mary's role as the mother of God by saying: "Blessed rather are those who hear the Word of God and keep it".

Some choose Mary as a mediator and to worship through, but Christ said: "You shall worship the Lord your God and Him only…" (Luke 4: 8; Deuteronomy 6: 5). Further "There is one God, and there is one mediator between God and men, the man Christ Jesus. I would recommend that you discard your rosary beads".

Enough said my friends. There have been beautiful women in history. There have been transformed women in history. There are beautiful women today; both created, and transformed. Maybe you are a beautiful mother, daughter, sister or wife. Look in the mirror and take an attitude check. Think about the women listed above. Read the books of Ruth and Esther, and then the Gospels. I might just throw in Proverbs 31: 10-31 for a close.

Be a beauty. It emanates from the inside out. The feeling is magnificent. The response is amazing. "But a woman who fears the Lord is to be praised" (Proverbs 31: 30).

Are You That Woman? Hang on; you are in for a great ride! ☺

Three Joys #5

To cut to the chase, as they say (I want to meet those people someday), there are three potential joys in this existence called life: Creation, salvation, and resurrection! If you were not created, then you would not be reading this "Brief". Since you are reading this, you either experienced, or can experience salvation in this life (Ephesians 2: 8, 9). At the end of it all you will be buried or burned, only to experience your personal resurrection (Daniel 12: 2).

Firstly, Creation! "It is I (God) who made the earth and created man upon it (Isaiah 45: 12)". I love the way my Creator, Lord, and Savior just slips these little verses in, to build my faith as I find them. The infinite, all-powerful Creator God brings it down to my level of comprehension. It is just like my daily practice of Googling questions with the seemingly infinite capability to answer from word definitions to the distance to Yuma, but not how many angels can fit on the head of a pin! ☺

My second Joy then is Salvation! Is that yours? Have you sinned at all in life? Have you broken any of the Big Ten (Commandments)? James 2: 10: "For whoever keeps the whole Law, and yet stumbles in one point, he/she has become guilty of all". Some people/Christians believe it is simply awful to steal, lie, or murder, and it is, but think nothing of disliking to hating their parents. James clears that up as God's standard is perfection, in everything. Corinthians 5: 17: "Therefore, if any man/woman is in Christ, he is a new creature; the old things passed away; behold, new things have come. It is true, it is real; ask a saved person who you trust".

My third Joy will be Resurrection! In Corinthians 15: 12, 13: "But if there is no resurrection of the dead, not even Christ has been raised". The question is posed in verse 12; if we are preaching it, it must be the case, or why would we preach it (Acts 24: 15)? "Having a hope in God…that there shall certainly be a resurrection of both the righteous and the wicked" (Reference Daniel 12: 2 again). Make sure that you are in the right group!

So now you get my personal focuses in my life. Are they your particular Joys? Are you happy you were born? Are you happy you got saved? Then you will be happily looking forward to your resurrection in the future. For years I have continually looked forward to my futures. I wanted to be a high school football player, and have children, who have blessed me richly. Did I mention my wife? Whoops; shoot par in golf, and have a fun, successful business experience. Now I have studied up on the subject and cannot wait for the Millennium. Why? Because the Bible records it for the future.

Let's not forget about heaven. Let's go back to golf again. If I shoot pars in the Millennium, then I anticipate birdies in Heaven. OK back to reality. I am every bit as excited about my future now, as I have been in my current life.

Would you care to join me? Get your joy together (as they say)!

Abide in Me #6

"Abide in Me, as I in you. As the branch cannot bear fruit of itself, unless it abides in the vine, neither can you, unless you abide in Me!" (John 15: 4)

If you have not looked at John 15 before, then just take a gander! Jesus (the radical) spells out to what faith produces. You would think that God created TV's and cell phones for today as a last hurrah! People believe they are of the Christian faith, but neglect to exercise their faith. I hate to beat the fellowship drum, but I am scared there are some (not) true believers out there fooling themselves.

Christ said "As the branch cannot bear fruit of itself, unless it "abides" in the vine, so neither can you, unless you abide in me" (Verse 4) Are you an active believer? Verse 6 notes that inactivity with fellow Christians (not abiding), leads to throwing away for burning. I do not like that inference/admonition;

 Do you?

This whole analogy of vines and branches made a lot of sense to people in an agrarian society. This was pre-beer days, and the only means for health and partying was a jug of wine. Get with the program dear reader, this is rubber meets the road theology. Jesus was great at that, just read the parables. Know this: I share this to encourage you, not to criticize. The whole program for faith in your Creator is to Repent, Accept Christ's Sacrifice for You, And Live It (Share It).

Christ says a lot in this chapter. If you read it 3 times, then you will see three new things. If you read it 10 times, then you will see ten. He notes in verse 16 that He chose us; as opposed to? Because of that He wrote in verse 19 that we are on a different trip in this world. He further states the world system/people will hate you.

Try it out this week. Tell your friends you were created by God! Tell your friend, then, you should not kill unborn babies. Tell your friends that sex comes after marriage and in marriage, only. Tell your friends not to get drunk, but be filled with the Holy Spirit!

I think you get the point. The Bible takes a dramatically different turn then what you hear from certain friends and school teachings. Christ was very social, and He asks that of us also. It is called fellowship from a Greek word ecclesia, and is noted in Chapters 2 and 3 of Revelation. It should be noted, however, that all those called out were not saved. Only those who "overcame" were saved. Only those who abided in Christ were saved.

In Matthew 7: 21-23, I find one of the scariest quotes Christ said: "I never knew you" That keeps me on edge, and active. The thought that I might reach eternity and have him say that to me, drives me to faith from the negative side. I encourage myself with all the positive verses and pastors who remind me. Nonetheless, I need to abide, and on that I focus. May I leave you line walkers with this:

Get Saved And Get Active!

Do Not Get Burned! ☹

After Life #7

One of the many questions of mankind in this life is what happens when one dies. For people who study, believe, and follow the Scriptures, the answer is clear. Once you have been created, you live forever! Before this "Brief" is completed, that will be made clear. If one asks God to forgive them, repents, and gets baptized, the answer leaps out. For one who is created, does not feel the need for forgiveness, and does not repent, they have no clue as to post-life existence.

The most famous section is in the New Testament is John 3: 16. Actually, you would do well to read verses 16- 21. It speaks of belief about both, who and what. It speaks of eternal life, truth, light, and darkness in this world and in one's person. It speaks of Love and judgment! It speaks of just how great God's Love is for His creation.

I live in, and associate with, people that live in a gated community for 55+ personages. I must propose, however, that the average age is +/- 70 years of age. By this time most have hardened into positions concerning politics, religion, and social life. Given the socio-economic level of the participants, they have spent most of their lives spending, saving, investing, and enjoying the attributes concurrent with a free society.

At this late stage, it is difficult to share with someone that they may be looking forward to an eternal existence in most unpleasant surroundings. Life has been too good for them to envision any prospect of punishment for faith or Creator rejection. Knowing your destiny is the result of faith in our Creator. If you do not know "where you are going", then I can tell you! But let's not depend on my opinion; let's go back to the Bible.

There is one group of people who feel that when you pass, you are buried, and cease to exist. There is another group that believes that you die from this life, and if you were not the best that you get another chance to work your way back up the change. There is another group which believes that you could purchase indulgences to insure your passing was a benefit. What does the Bible say? "It is appointed for men to die once, and after this comes judgment" (Hebrews 9: 27). How could an unconscious person be judged?

"And many of those who sleep in the dust of the ground will awake, these to everlasting life, but the others to disgrace and everlasting contempt" (Daniel 12: 2). Going into dirt my friend, is a stopping point on the way to resurrection it says. "If anyone's name was not written in the Book of Life, he was thrown into the Lake of Fire" (Revelation 20: 15). Chapter 21 speaks of the New Heaven and Earth and states "He who overcomes shall inherit these things, and I will be his God and he will be My son" (Revelation 21: 7).

So look ahead, and plan like I have dear reader. A loving God and Creator seeks your acceptance (John 1: 12). Not everyone is God's child. Become a part of the family, today, and look forward to enjoying your afterlife. ☺

Bad Samaritan #8

Just about everyone in this culture has heard of the "good Samaritan" at some time or another. At least church people have in a sermon or two. A Jewish lawyer asked Christ whom he should love, and Christ said "love your neighbor" (The story is recorded in Luke 10: 25-37). The lawyer then asked who was his neighbor and Christ related the unexpected. Jesus suggested (?) that his neighbor was none other than a stranger in need. It was a culture thing back then as to who one was supposed to like or love; sort of like asking a Yankee fan to love a Red Sox fan; only worse!

So where did I get my title to this "1 Page Brief"? I was on my way to church one Saturday past when a car was blocking our lane with a green light showing. Of course that is frustrating, and especially when you are on your way to church with a well-practiced smile for love-sharing. Please forgive the mild sarcasm, as I only hope to make the point. I really do enjoy seeing friends and experiencing Christian fellowship.

Back to the traffic jam! Some poor lady was stopped in a rather dirty old sedan, which had obviously quit running. She was stuck! The thought passed my consciousness to stop and assist her from her travail, but I was a bit late for my Christian fellowship and was sure some "good" Samaritan would assist, or assuredly she had a cell phone to call for aide. So like the Priest or the Levite in the parable, I passed on the other side and made it to my religious experience on time. Hopefully this "Brief" will finally expunge my guilt.

Let me firstly submit that I have stopped in the past to change a tire or give a ride. It brings enormous satisfaction to the psyche or soul, and actually helps one in need. The idea of helping a stranger as a fellow human being, is the "love your neighbor" action Christ was defining. God loved me: "while I was still a sinner" (Romans 5: 8). The Good Samaritan loved his neighbor; unrequested. He went further by attending to the victim's needs, including all the costs involved. For the sake of this Jewish lawyer, Jesus identified this gracious helper as a Samaritan.

So as a "Bad Samaritan" that day, I exhort you, and myself, do not pass by. Give a helping hand to someone who may seem/be helpless. Experience the love action of which Christ speaks. I guarantee a great feeling that lasts…

Be A Good Samaritan ☺

Be Crucified #9

Wow, that is a tough one. It shrieks with giving up any power in life and letting it all go to your cross. I do not think the average person begins to realize what Christ gave up to come into this life and make that sacrifice. Do you remember how He left the earth? In Acts 1, He shot up in the air, unattended, and unaided, to prove His power was back. His mission was over, and the die was cast for the future and salvation of mankind. He did not get on a plane and take off, He just took off. Christ had solved the greatest conflict of all time, between the created, and the Creator.

In men's fellowship this May weekend, Pastor Curtis covered the topic of solving conflicts. The text was out of James 4. What is the source of quarrels and conflicts among you? Is not the source your pleasures that wage war in your members? It then goes on to mention murder, covetousness, and adultery. It continues with love for the world system of success, coupled to the engine of pride. We are exhorted to "Draw therefore to God. Resist the devil and he will flee from you".

When was the last time you entered a conflict seeking to be crucified? Have you done that with an athletic competitor, with a business competitor, with a spouse? I did not turn the other cheek in football, ever, or I would have been the water boy. In business I won the contract to insure I kept my position. Marriage (24/7) can be the ultimate challenge. If you do not believe that, then check with all my divorced friends.

So I believe God was speaking to a different focus on conflict, and one's attitude! My pleasures? If getting through this life is motivated by personal satisfaction and pleasure, then the trip can be odious. As I write this "Brief", a movie star named Johnny Depp and his former wife are fighting in court over fifty million dollars. Now if $50MM will not satisfy you, or buy you pleasure, what amount will? So why do we fight? We want to win and be pleasured according to James.

What is the answer then to personal satisfaction? Be crucified! Verses 13-17 cover it well. In my business career, I had 15 difficult years from age twenty five to forty. I was marginally talented, educated, enthusiastic, and driven. It paid off in the end, but it was no cake walk during the process. Paul's walk of jail time, beatings, stoning, and shipwrecks as listed in second Corinthians 11: 23-28 to exemplify his sacrificial ministry. Christ's crucifixion makes no sense to me as a human being, but is a part of God's process and selflessness.

God, the Son, had the power, and gave it up. Paul had the power, and gave it up. My goal then is not to gain that power, but to give it up. The Bible promises enormous power, pleasure, and satisfaction in the end. Read Revelation 21 & 22. The Book of Isaiah is laced with promises of eternal life and peace. Do I really need to win that argument for turf and pleasure with my fellow worker or spouse? "Choose this day whom you will serve..." (Joshua 24: 15).

Do you want a healthy, happy, career and marriage? I suggest you cop a positive attitude early my friend:

Be Crucified!

Beautification Of The Believer #10

As I approached our church last weekend, I noticed a sign in the small pit by the entrance way to our buildings. I snickered at first notice, and then thought, hey, that would be a good "Brief". The "committee" has been busy the last few months fixing up the previous estate to accommodate the growth in attendance from 1 to 5 services. New branch church plants, and the accompanying growth in family church schools for all the new kiddies are also being accounted for.

Whatever God has in His plans, it is nothing new, but it is new to this fellowship. It is growing, it is fun to be a part of, and I cannot wait to see the ministry-arms extend. I told the two initial pastors that they could expect significant growth in the near future, and when asked why, I stated because I was there. I had to pick them back up as they fell down laughing (and rightly so). My point is that over the years, I have been attracted to fellowships that seem to attract active Christians. It is happening!

The sign: Beautification In Progress

Paul wrote to the Church at Philippi 1: 6: "He who began a good work in you will perfect it until the day of Christ Jesus". I believe this to be the exciting affirmation for all born-again believers as to where salvation initiated, and how it is processed. God is involved "all the way". We side-step repeatedly, but He never tears up the blueprints. Much of the work on our building reformation is done, leaving this gaping mud hole at the entrance to it all. I suggested a new baptismal, but they stuck this sign in it to minister the message.

So what is our part? Philippians 2: 12: "work out your own salvation with fear and trembling". So we are not just a bunch of nebbishes. We actually have a role in this beautification process. The saying I heard was "do not ask God to guide your steps, if you are not moving your feet". My counselor would like that one! What does that great economic energizer proliferate? "Just Do It". And why? "For it is God who is at work in you, both to will and to work for His good pleasure".

So there you have it dear reader, His part and ours. How is you beautification process going? It has to be active and planned. It must include active God faith. The message of Solomon's Ecclesiastes book is that life lived and planned without God is "meaningless or vanity at best". He concluded with "fear God and keep His commandments" (Ecclesiastes 12: 13).

Just do it!

Becoming Interactive #11

I would think that one of the immediate responses to salvation would be fellowship. In two of my earlier briefs, I have labeled the trinities of churches and individuals. They both have the triangle "point" of "fellowship" as one of the descriptive elements/personalities of the triune gatherings/personalities. In my gated community each week, management emails a list of fellowship activities for potential entertainment and community fellowship. It seems to be an inborn trait for people.

In 1 John 1: 7 we read: "if we walk in the light as He Himself is in the light, we have fellowship with one another". It would seem natural then that salvation leads to fellowship with other Christians. Then why do I have relatives that profess to be saved, but do not attend church or share in Bible study share-groups? Are (Matthew 7: 23) they really saved, or are they just religious? I actually dislike/hate that verse where Christ said "I never knew you" to those who practiced the Christian religion, but whom apparently were never truly saved.

So becoming interactive with other Christians, stimulates our faith, and helps us grow. It takes effort and participation. As Bible study, prayer, and fellowship are intertwined, we see the "stimulation" mentioned and encouraged in Hebrews 10: 24, 25. I just studied Mark 4: 1-20 on the parable of the sower. Were some of us fooled? Were we born into a Christian family, thinking our salvation came with the package? This does happen, and children eventually dislike their parents, and even consider their parents to be hypocrites when they see the sins in their parent's nature and lives.

David once complained when he lost a friend, as opposed to fighting an enemy. He said "we who had sweet fellowship together" (Psalm 55: 14). Paul refers to the "fellowship of the Holy Spirit", as he concludes the Book of second Corinthians 13: 14. So fellowship than seems not to be referred to as an option, but rather a mandate. It is descriptive of a relationship that is a result of salvation. With all the

TV watchers today, we may be witnessing a tide of "cheap" salvations. All sincere preachers or evangelists always suggest people to immediately join and participate in local fellowship.

I think, at this point, you can see I believe fellowship to be a mandate for expressing fellowship with fellow believers. The alternative is to be with non-believers or just sit in front of a TV and be educated and fed more of the "worldly" program. So for me, it is a mandate:

 Get active! With Christians!

Being Born Twice #12

Sounds weird, does not it? That is what a guy named Nicodemus thought two thousand years ago. He was a member of the local leadership in his church and had asked the man Jesus, what he was talking about. Christ was explaining the process necessary to qualify for a trip to heaven. Heaven? That is one of the two alternatives for eternal travel at the end of this existence (death). People, who plan on that eternal trip, realize the qualification and are excited. The people who are ignorant of their destiny, ignore the subject, and at worst, ignore the issue!

Pastor Jon expounded on John 3: 4-7 in his message. He taught on the concept of birth and what it is all about. Why did Christ use the symbolism of birth? It is very simply that we should take as much pride in that event of Spiritual birth as we did in our physical birth. Are you proud of being saved as opposed to your neighbor's rejection of salvation? Did you feel like your salvation was like hitting the lottery? Did you feel that way about your physical birth?

It is weird when you reach that point of realization, and I will finally explain it to you after we take that giant step of transition (death). In the meantime, I will still approach the subject just like Christ did with his contemporary Nicodemus. Whatever it takes, whatever the process, no matter your involvement, you must be "born again", to get into God's Kingdom. Get It? If you are reading this, affirm it, or "Do It"!

By the way, I believe this Nicodemus "Did It". He later participated in Christ's burial, after the crucifixion. Given his priestly position, he could have lost a lot of face in the community for that action. I might add it was expensive. In John 19: 39 and 40, we read that he used 100 pounds of myrrh and wrapped up the body of Christ. Do you have any doubt based on that record that the body of Jesus was dead? I do not think so. For three days, that body was not functioning my friend.

So that is the message! It took Jon an hour (and it was well spent); I try to do it in a page. You have got to be born twice. Once for your body, and mind, and once for your Spirit! Ask God. Receive His Spirit! You will love the ride, and the eventual promised payoff!

 Get Born Again!

Breathe Each Day #13

That is how it all began, if you believe the Bible. Genesis 2: 7 "Then the Lord God formed man of the dust from the ground, and breathed into his nostrils the breath of life; and man became a living being". Now you can take that version, or if you do not believe in God, you can take Darwin's version and check out your great granddaddy at the zoo. I prefer the biblical creation myself.

Job got into that in his book right before the Psalms. His faith was allowed to be tested by God's adversary, and Job lost his family and fortune and exclaimed: "I waste away, I will not live forever, leave me alone, for my life is but a breath". He later stated in Job "For as long as life is in me, and the breath of God is in my nostrils, my lips certainly will not speak unjustly nor will my tongue utter deceit".

So there seems to be more than one kind of breath coming from our mouths. One is from God, one is from us. From the unsaved, however, it is only from us. I told a good friend the other day to "take a breath". Or, I might add, "Just Breathe"! I face that issue personally, and fight the problem of being verbose, in person, which is my issue; thus my "1 Page Briefs". With these briefs, I can get to the point, calm the verbosity, and remove the element of physical imposition.

In David's final verse of Praise He said "Let everything that has breath praise the Lord" (Psalm 150: 6). Let your words come from the Lord, think of the Lord, and assuredly be given in a manor to Praise The Lord". What if you have a significant need to be heard, to be loved, to be felt? Express yourself in more than one way. Of course you will speak, but how about writing something down, and also, How About A Hug?

So if God is the Creator of our breath, as the Bible states, why not take a breath; for him. Do not be too silent, but also do not be overly verbose; Take A Breath. In Paul's sermon on Mars Hill, he said about God, the Creator, "neither is He served by human hands, as though He needed anything, since He Himself gives to all life and breath and all things…"

If God is the source of life and breath take time to breathe Him in, and then breathe Him out. If you do not breathe Him in, then you will not be breathing Him out. We are often times reminded in counseling, coaching, and preaching, that we have two ears and one mouth, for God-given reasons. Used in that proportion, you will be appreciated by all with whom you converse. Reverse that process, and you will pass through this existence alone!

God Bless You. Keep breathing! But for God's sake (and yours): Take A Breath!

Climate Change #14

The latest attack on the creative God of the Universe as detailed in the Holy Bible is climate change. Godless prognosticators in the current world are looking forward at a flooded world as they see diminishing polar ice, and as they imagine the disappearance of the all-white polar bears. They totally neglect the population surge from 1-8 BB people in the world, and people are 75% water. They totally ignore the vast quantities of water backed up and saved (?) from the recycling system of water causing the need for new sources of replenishment. For more extensive details you can be read about it in the book: "Climategate" by Brian Sussman.

The Bible notes the beginning (creation) of the world at the Bible's beginning! In Genesis 1: 1, we read "In the beginning, God created the Heavens and the Earth!" The Bible also reveals the ending of this creation and development in 2 Peter 3 "But the day of the Lord will come like a thief, in which the heavens will pass away with a roar and the elements will be destroyed with intense heat, and the earth and its works will be burned up". Most Christians do not know this; no unbelievers do!

That is why non-believers in God and the Bible created theory of evolution. That is why non-believers in God and the Bible also think in terms of millions and billions of years. They cannot deal with life ending in the future or with any short term period (1000s of years) of existence. Now let's get to the latest creative fantasy: mankind is responsible for the climate. If we do not end the use of fossil fuels, then we will pollute ourselves to death and the ocean waters will rise and drown us.

Christ had a short-term solution for that premise. Please read Mark 4: 35-41. As Christ and the disciples crossed the Sea of Galilee, a storm came up. The small fishing vessel was tossed, and the fishermen knew they were doomed. Christ was sleeping in the back of the boat on a cushion. He was mad that they woke Him up and He was upset. Christ then said to the storm: "Hush be still". The wind died down and became perfectly still. To the disciples, He said: "How is it that you have no faith?"

So there you have it again. To argue with truth, mankind continues to come up with ideas to contradict the Bible. Evolution instead of Creation! Life for billions more years instead of finality and judgment! And lastly, man-made climate change instead of God-controlled weather. I think I will stick with the Bible. Let the non-believers chase and activate their fantasies.

Have A Sunny Day! ☺

"Coincidence" In The Scripture #15

In a Bible study recently, Marcos said the word is not found in the Scripture: the Bible. So to support his declaration, I perused my Strong's exhaustive concordance and Bible dictionary. He came up empty for that word. I then Googled it and gained this definition: "A remarkable occurrence of events or circumstances without apparent causal connection". Get it? Causal connection!

Nothing happens in this created life that God has not touched with His fingers (if you will)! That is what we see in the Bible. "When I consider the Heavens, the work of Your fingers" (Psalm 8: 3). "Before I formed you in the womb, I knew you" (Jeremiah 1: 5). "For I know the plans that I have for you!" (Jeremiah 29: 11). "I am the Alpha and the Omega, the First and the Last, the Beginning and the End" (Revelation 22: 13).

The learning challenge for a believer who places their faith and trust in God Almighty, and the creation of Heaven and Earth, (Genesis 1: 1), is to gradually expunge the word "coincidence" from their vocabulary. It is very difficult in an educated society. We are the masters of our own destiny, even though we are born helpless. We take pride in our riches, even though we are told prosperity is a gift in Ecclesiastes 7: 14. After years of education from our culture in training, it is difficult to go Biblical. But it is there!

To me personally, the counter word to coincidence is Faith. It is defined and exemplified in Hebrews 11. "Now faith is the assurance of things hoped for, the conviction of things not seen". Well excuse Me!!! Assurance, Conviction, in what? I do not think for a second, any more, that the Bible is silly, stupid, or ridiculous. But I do know more than a few people that are, have been, or will be in my life and in my mirror.

So if you think riches are your greatness, physical stature or girth is to be proud of, IQ is earned, Rulers and politicians earn their position, without Godly intervention, you should start to read God's Word. He covers it all, from womb to tomb. He covers it all from birth to death. The Word covers it all, from Creation, to Eternity.

Check it out! ☺☹

"Confession!" The Mark Of The True Believer #16

When I say the "mark", do you get the point? In the book of Revelation, we read about the "Mark of the beast". This permanent ID is taken on at a time when one will not be able to buy or sell without it (Revelations 13). Young people "mark" themselves with tattoos now, implanting permanent ink in pictures under their skin. People line up for vaccines today, cursing those who will not, in the face of the latest pandemic.

So having a mark, in flesh or in Spirit, is a permanent covenant of faith to our Savior or the system (culture). It is either confession or license. My point here is that the way human beings line up for instruction or control makes much more sense out of Christ referring to us as sheep. I take significant umbrage to Christians criticizing Christians as in sheep fighting sheep! What a stupid notion! Ignorance attacking ignorance! It makes me think of the end of John's gospel (John 21: 22) when Peter approached Christ about John. Christ as much as said "mind your own business", "You Follow Me"!

Confession or Criticism? To me, that is the choice. Now I do not condone false theology and will be the first to defend Jesus as God in the flesh (1John 5: 1-13). I will stand up and hold the Nicaean Creed in hand. However, one Christian denomination fighting against another gets a little bit sketchy. Some go way too far with prosperity, glossolalia, and healing, but most egregious is the constant appeal to offerings for the ministry. Television and cell phones have added to the hype today. Preaching was formerly a vow of poverty. But, not anymore!

So what does confession accomplish? You bring God into the picture. We are admonished to: "confess me before men" (Matthew 10: 32), "confessing their sins" (Mark 1: 5). If we confess our sins, then He is faithful and just to forgive us our sins and cleans us from ALL unrighteousness" (1 John 1: 9). We are going to our Creator guys, and asking for forgiveness in a truly repentant Spirit.

I crossed a line years ago and confessed. I crossed a line awhile back and sincerely worked at repenting (Turning, turning, turning around). I really crossed a line recently, and sold out, as they say! Adam and Eve are real historic people. Noah built the Arc and the atmosphere changed. Daniel entered the Lion's den, and King Nebuchadnezzar witnessed it. Christ died in the flesh on the cross, and rose in the flesh three days later. The end of this world is coming soon, just like Israel re-arose and sits in the Middle East as prophesied. Because I confessed, and repented, and chose to get baptized:

I Am Going To Heaven When I Fall Asleep; Finally! ☺

Discernment #17

The Ability To Judge Well

Need I say more? Absolutely! There are two extremes for this point of definition for a Biblical reasoning; "the distinguishing of Spirits", to the baseline of distinguishing nothing. Have you met these two types? The Christian faith is loaded with all kinds of personalities, and the stronger ones seem outspoken, and the weaker ones are not. Every true born-again believer has a role, and it is good to search those out and exercise them. See my "Brief" on exercise!

 They are all listed in 1 Corinthians 12, and Romans 12 (I will bet God set those 12's up). He compares the gifts to body parts. Which part of your body is the most important? Arms when you are lifting? Eyes when you are seeing? Legs when you are walking? Lungs when you are breathing? It goes on and on. Which live part is activated in fellowship by you? Which dead body part is dead and separated from Christian fellowship because you refuse to attend church, get fed (taught and exhorted), and help your body to function (fellowship)?

I think discernment is very important. Many fellowships however, focus on differences. All Christians focus on Jesus Christ, and the Triune Godhead. Many Christians focus on how to worship, how to baptize, and on which day to have church; to name only a few. That is why we have denominations, schools, and seminaries celebrating the "correct" theologies. I see why Christ picked fishermen!

So discernment is one of the "listed" Spiritual gifts. It is a part of the body. It is the ability to see a false Spirit in the body who might be leading the weaker parts/people, to a false position. The easier ones to detect are those who reject Christ coming in the flesh as noted in 1John 4: 2, and 1John 5: 4, 5. The danger here is those castigating others they do not like personally, or a person who disagrees with them due to weak, poor, or less educated theology.

I have been asked to leave three fellowships in my last fifty years, and I do not take that personally. I have a large frame and am outspoken as I learn. This has rubbed people the wrong way, and as an ex-football lineman, I tend to edge on insensitivity as I shirk the need to turn my other cheek. In that sense, it is not a proud moment, especially, when I know more, and therefore "should" know better. But in all instances, I was being called to a new assignment which physically necessitated a move away. In other words, I was blessed.

So if in fellowship, find someone with discernment! They will help the fellowship grow in the Spirit as they help to remove the weeds from your beautiful garden. If the climates right:

Go Grow Some Roses ☺

Do As I Say….Not As I Do #18

Have you ever thought this? Have you ever said this? Have you ever taught this? Matthew covers the topic in detail. Christ was confronting the Pharisees and scribes for their hypocrisy. He knew His time had come, as He was in "His" last days. If He got them mad/angry enough, then they would go to the Roman rulers, and have Him crucified. Christ knew all this, and He knew the plan. His disciples however just did not get what He literally told them. "Destroy this building (His body) and I will rebuild it in three days" (John 2: 19).

In Matthew 23, we see Christ lambasting the Jewish leadership aggressively. He calls them phonies and hypocrites. They dress up, wear prayer boxes, and expensive robes with prayer tassels. He calls them out for wearing these ostentatious outfits to the marketplace, just to be seen. He criticizes their tithing (giving and tax payments) noting the extremes they go to. He called them on visiting widows, guess what for? He stated they strained gnats from drinking water, but ate the camel (That is cultural, in a region where camels were the local Uber ride). He was not nice!

That was only a partial list, but it worked. They were mad and they took it out on him. One other thing, He instructed His disciples not to use the terms Rabbi, father, or teacher to aggrandize these phonies. He instructed His disciples to save those appellations for God the father, and Christ. It is interesting today that the Jewish religion uses "Rabbi", and the Catholics use "Father". One of my pastors processed this to mean the end of these titles for modern usage. I am concerned about the "pick and choose" of that analysis, given the use of teacher in Paul's Epistles, but it is not a hill to die on.

So what is Christ communicating here? I think the conclusion is obvious to me. Do Not Be A Phony (hypocrite). Do not study and believe everything from the Ten Commandments to the Sermon on the Mount, and drown in the culture; drinking, carousing, divorcing, lying, cheating, getting rich, murdering, etc. Live out what you study and believe from the Scriptures. I believe a study of the Book of James will clarify that teaching.

The challenge is not to learn the Scriptures, but, instead, it is to live the Scriptures. I have spent unfortunate periods experiencing the culture that I live in, even after salvation. I am sorry, but it is hard. My pastor/counselor sees thirty or forty people a week who share those thoughts and actions as the Pharisees (do not be prideful). But I do not have to be a hypocrite. Shoot for the moon, and higher. Do not give in. Read verses; daily.

Be real! The best is yet to come! And I plan on being there (Revelation 21, 22). ☺

Do Not Complain (Bitch) #19

There was a period early on in the Exodus, where the people were complaining to Moses because of the conditions they faced. They had left Egypt, were loaded down with Gold and Silver, had passed through the Red Sea, seen Pharaohs army destroyed as it chased them, and still did not see God's hand in the activity. They lamented "Why have you brought us up out of Egypt to die in the desert? For there is no food and no water, and we loath this miserable food" (Numbers 21: 5).

I chuckled as I read/heard this at church, being offered to compare our faith in Christ, as we look up to and accept His sacrifice for our sins. The people were attacked by venomous serpents, and God had Moses erect a bronze statue with a snake affixed, so that when Israelites was bitten, they could look up at the bronze snake and live. Christ compared that to his sacrifice on the cross that we could look up to and be saved (John 3: 14).

Why did I chuckle, you ask? About 9 years ago, I moved my wife to the Arizona desert. We had lived in South California, near the ocean. Need I say more? We knew no one, had no church in which to fellowship, did not know any good restaurants, and the first summer of heat was horrendous. My wife was not really happy, and except for the golf, I was not pleased as well! But that is where God drew me! Today we have great church, great friends, and a list of restaurants we cannot possibly attend to!

After the message was preached by Jon, I leaned over to my wife, and suggested that we check the front porch at home to insure no venomous snakes were lurking about. Now I am the first to say that given the summer months, Arizona is not the God-send of environments. The balance of the year, however, is a major offset of weatherly delight.

I think what I hope and wish to convey, however, is that God has a purpose for one living wherever He places them. I could have been born and raised in central Mexico, Venezuela, Russia, or China. Would I have been saved, or what if I had been saved? I think you get the picture. The challenge in this life than is to be grateful to our Creator, and especially for our salvation. How can one complain at being raised in this country, in these suburbs, in Christian homes, in freedom? But people do!

I think we need to focus on thanksgiving, day and night, until we get the picture. As Paul wrote "In everything give thanks, for this is God's will for you in Christ Jesus" (1 Thessalonians 5: 18).

Look out for them snakes!

Do Not Pull The Nails From His Hands Or His Feet #20

Do not pull the Nails from His Hands or His Feet.

Each pounding of pain leads to my peaceful sleep.

As He took on my sins in this Glorious task,

Beyond human reason; how could I have asked?

Each day I am selfish, each day I proclaim:

It is my satisfaction that I later disdain!

Be it willful or not, it is, none-the-less

My daily thoughts, against what, I know best.

So why do I try, to pull nails from His feet,

It is a belief in my time, for my sins; self-defeat.

His glory allows for His pain, in my stead,

To pull nails from the Cross would pour coals on my head.

Dear Jesus, Sweet Jesus, your name I proclaim.

To my so small world, thanks be for your pain.

How silly, but human, my grief given you,

When it is me that needs pity, for all that I do.

So the nails as I pound them, with all my disdain,

For what I do wrongly, and not rightly proclaim;

Leave them in and God save, for a life unto you,

Eternity calls, and I will pursue.

The nails are but symbols of my fall away

You sacrificed yes, for me on that tree.

The nails you removed; with no help from me,

When you passed from this life, for eternity!

And a promise I hold by the pain of your loss,

Is to join you myself when it is my turn to cross.

Jim Shafer

June 2015

Dress For Success #21

Man did that kick in a load of memories. Pastor Dave shared the Scripture out of Colossians at men's fellowship this AM. As he shared behind the lectern wearing a $3.50 T-shirt, he posted a power point showing John T. Molloy's 1970's book on how to dress for success. I lived that book! Starting in the mid 60's, I shopped on the Chicago Magnificent Mile, and decked out for my future sales positions. Back then in my 6'2", 200# ex-football frame, to be nattily dressed was an asset. First Impressions in sales, ya know! I also belonged to a very nice Country Club, and blue jeans were not allowed.

The whole point being shared by Dave was extracted from Colossians 3: 12-15. The stress was placed on the inner clothing, and not the outer fibers. We do not live in an age where clothing means what it was in the past. The average guy in Arizona shows up in shorts and a T-shirt, and half of us work out of our house. Need I say more?

So coming to the collected church, is not what it used to be. Many Christians (?) see the church gathering on TV or a computer screen. The public adornment items include tight pants and out-hanging shirts. Shirts and ties are for attorneys and accountants. Casual day has long since become a Monday through Friday routine. So how do you outshine your fellow parishioners?

I think/know that God handles it aptly in James 2. That is correct; the whole chapter. It is hard not to have an attitude when you have been blessed materially. I have been lucky! I have played golf for fifty years and have been on courses from Miami to Seattle, and from San Diego to Maine. I have been to Europe a dozen times, Hawaii, China, Israel, Mexico, and Hawaii. But every time I could have made it big in business; I did not. What a blessing! My autobiography is entitled "The Edge of Greatness".

Because of my failures in the vicinity of riches however, I have grown spiritually while I went broke. I have been driven to the Scripture and Christian fellowship, as I was driven to the periodic poor house. Now,

I am not destitute my friend, but I have been desperate. In these processes I have learned as did Paul: "to preach…, the unfathomable riches of Christ" (Ephesians 3: 8). As the old tale goes: "I have never seen a hearse with a U-Haul trailer attached". It is like the guy who showed up in heaven with two bags of gold, and was asked how long he planned on carrying those bags of pavement around?

Dress for Success? Colossians 3: 12-15: "put on (dress) with compassion, kindness, humility, gentleness, and patience…bearing with one another, forgiving each other, No Complaints, forgive as God forgave you"! Wow, I would like to find that church. Maybe with the attendant Pastoral encouragement like this preachment, I already have. ☺

Is God Your Haberdasher?

Dying For Christ #22

I recently was rereading the biography of Dietrich Bonhoeffer written by Eric Metaxas. Author Metaxas labeled him as Pastor, Martyr, Prophet, and spy. It is not that Bonhoeffer was a great man per se', but he was outstanding for the time in which he lived, the 1930's and 1940's. He was from Germany and as a born-again Christian, knew Hitler to be maniacal and antichrist. Because Bonhoeffer participated in Hitler's assassination plot, he was placed in prison for two years and finally hanged. The irony was that he was transferred and hanged within three weeks of the Americans arriving at his death camp.

My son-in-law's mother lived through the Hitler years as a teenager, and the war ending bombings that completely decimated German cities through 1945. I was a baby and young lad essentially unscathed by that war in which 60-80 million people were killed by Stalin and Hitler. Bonhoeffer left Germany to teach and preach in England and the USA during the late 30's and early 40's. He returned to do what he could as his Christian conscience drove him home.

Metaxas quoted Bonhoeffer "We must look only at God, and in Him we are reconciled to our situation in the world". Was that not what Abraham did? How about Moses, or Gideon, or David facing Goliath? Or Daniel, or Jeremiah, or John the Baptist, or the Apostles, or Paul? How many over history have turned in faith to their Creator and sustainer? And Today? How about Christians in Russia, or China, or Sudan, or any Muslim country? How about young children in our public schools who are taught one thing at home and in Sunday school only to be mocked and tormented in the school halls?

People are dying for their faith everywhere today in our God-forsaken world. Our faith in the veracity of the Holy Bible is not shared by 80% of the world's peoples. In our own free country, schools have ceased to train up children Biblically. The Founders did. They had Bible study in the Nation's Capital. The Bible was the chief Primer in the schools. Harvard, Yale, and Princeton, were seminaries.

We were fighting for the freedom to worship God our Creator. We were "endowed by our Creator, with life, liberty, and the pursuit of happiness" as the Founders so aptly stated in our Declaration of Independence.

I make no excuses for my privilege in life. I have been raised in, and lived in the suburbs all my life. I have passed through, but never been sequestered in major city ghettos. I missed the Vietnam War due to color blindness. I passed through the poor areas of Mexico, visited East Berlin behind the wall, but never experienced prison. My awareness of persecution is from Bible stories from history, and the "Voice of the Martyrs" books in the present.

The world system is both beautiful and ugly. We are presently on a path with war conflicts, weather, and drought. We live in a society that has moved away from family and natural gender, and murders its unborn children out of convenience. Take up the mantel dear reader. Try and live the Ten Commandments. Love your neighbor and your enemy. Live your life to give, and not just get. Be careful, however, because the way the World is turning, in the near future you might be asked personally to:

Die For Your Faith In Christ!

Easter: A Day Of Worship #23

What a joy for me last Sunday. I go to church services like some people attend baseball games. Different strokes for different folks. Let me share my exuberance:

I heard firstly from Pastor Jon. He spoke of Christ's sacrifice as we focused on John 3. The story goes that a world pandemic had hit and a pure-blooded person needed to give a few pints which would become a vaccine and save "the World". That person was found but turned out to be a young lad. His parents had to sign him over to save the world. Would you? I think of this young lad, and I think of Isaac, and I think of Jesus. Resurrection day is really about the potential/reality of one's ultimate sacrifice.

I was driven to memory of my firstborn who died after three days. We were asked to donate John for research on his physical malady, and will never know how many babies were saved based on our/his sacrifice. The latest statistic is almost 200,000/year as it is now treatable. He died due to being born with Hyaline Membrane Disease. He is the first person my wife and I wish to meet in heaven.

Secondly, Pastor Costi shared first Peter 3: 3-5. It basically emphasizes how Jesus "caused us to be born again in a living "Hope" through the resurrection of Jesus Christ from the dead. I have friends who live without Hope. Some are down-trodden, some depressed, some just plain unhappy. If they could focus on "Hope", as Costi and Peter shared, then it is the trip out.

Thirdly, Pastor Chuck focused on the Bible location of Mark 5. Talk about Hope, starting with verse 21, the woman with blood issues said "If I just touched His garments, I shall get well". She did, and she did get well! A Jewish official asked Christ to heal his daughter. His hope was focused. Christ visited the little girl and she was healed. Hope matters my reader, but it is "who" you place your Faith and Hope in. If hope is just personally focused, then it will drain. If it is in the eternal, then it will grow and flourish as a seed or a bouquet. Try it, you will like it!

Pastor Dave was the icing on the cake. He used Christ's reference to Jonah. His story referred to the grade school girl who listened to her teacher's lesson on whales. After the teacher expounded on this great fish/animal, the 8 year old mentioned the Bible story of Jonah. The teacher responded on the silliness of that tale, since whales have too small a throat. The little girl said that she would ask Jonah when she got to heaven and the teacher responded: what if Jonah goes to hell. The little girl responded: "then you can ask him". ☺

Dave's teaching was Christ's point. I am going down for three days, but do not worry, I am resurrecting (Matthew 12: 40). And, that my friend, is what we are celebrating each April: The Resurrection!

So what is this whole personal achievement focus in America that we are trained in? We spend our first couple years having our diapers changed. Most of us spend our last couple years doing it again. Are we really masters of our own destiny? Why not seek, yield to, and worship our Creator. It is not bunnies and Easter eggs my friend, it is the Cross. And after the cross, it is the resurrection. So follow my team coaches (pastors) with me, and give Sacrifice, have Hope, and have Faith, and lastly, enjoy:

 Your resurrection!

Easter Or Resurrection Day? #24

It is amazing what we take for granted in our holidays and habit patterns. It has been an historic action for societies to cover pagan holiday celebrations with Christian celebrations. The problem always arises that the non-believers just cannot handle the swap. Resurrection day is no exception. Let's gain some knowledge.

Easter sounds a lot like Ishtar, the goddess of love, war, and sex. When Christianity took over the Roman Empire, she needed to be covered up. You could go to the Ishtar temple in those days and have some legal sex. That was their form of worship. If you are enticed by that potential, then I have a Pastor for you to visit. It is a manifestation, however of how we think in the flesh, and nothing is new. Please check out the stories of the Patriarchs, Samson, David, Solomon, and Hosea, as examples.

So plastic eggs have no connection to Jesus (other than He created them), and cute little rodent bunnies are noted for their prolific reproduction and Ishtar loved them.

P.S: they do not create eggs or poop them.

Your sidewalk is living proof. The hallmark of Christ's death then is the cross. The reality of His giving is the penalty He suffered at Golgotha, for me and you. But the beauty of the program is His return:

Christ's Resurrection!

So I am not a stick in the mud, but a historian. We really need to be careful of our noted celebrations. When you get cards or pictures from friends and relatives with bunnies and eggs instead of a cross and a cloud, maybe they missed the lesson in Sunday school. I will guarantee that they do not know the history lesson. Every year, they have an Easter egg hunt at the nation's capital. I will guarantee you that the nation's founders did not.

So enjoy the season! Enjoy the celebration! Just make sure you include a:

 Cross and a Cloud

Ecclesiastes Turn, Turn, Turn # 25

FIRST 10 YEARS   LAST 10 YEARS

So this life is a period of time. It begins and it ends. Two old men were chatting one day as the first complained of his aches and pains. The second said he felt like a newborn baby. When the first asked for an explanation, he answered, "I do not have any hair, I do not have any teeth and I think that I just wet my pants.

I came up with this image of life recently, as pictured like a bell curve. Teachers formally used this symbol to grade students. A few made A's, and a few made F's, and the balance filled the upper shell. I have now broken life down to decades; ten-year periods. Experiences tend to parallel on the upswing and downswing. The extreme would be pant-wetting. If you do not get it, then have or care for a baby. Then go visit a nursing home for a day. You will comprehend!

In 1 Corinthians 13: 11 Paul wrote: "When I was a child, I used to speak as a child, think as a child, and reason as a child". Can you remember your first ten years? Your parents can. They fed you, cleaned you, wiped you, and protected you. David gives you seventy years in Psalm 90: 10 (3 score and 10). The latest statistics is seventy eight years. It is that last 10 that get to you. At some point before death knocks on your door, someone will feed you, clean you, wipe you, and protect you. Do you get the cycle?

Back in 1959, Pete Seeger wrote lyrics to Solomon's song in the Scripture. Ecclesiastes 3 was the source, and the Byrd's made a hit in 1965. It paralleled to the nasty Vietnam War where over 50,000 young men lost their lives. How appropriate: a time to be born, and a time to die. Those are the two extremes of each of our lives. My picture of the entirety of life then is the bell we fill.

A time to plant and harvest, kill and heal, weep and laugh, mourn and dance, embrace and shun it, keep and throw away, be silent and a time to speak, a time to love and a time to hate, a time to war and a time for peace, and a few more (Ecclesiastes 3: 1-10). It goes so far as to say an "appointed time" as a beginning. In verse 10 he speaks of these appointed times as God appointed times to occupy us in this brief life! With that, we fill the bell curve of our existence from birth to death.

The key for me is, at some point, to have included my Creator in the process. He calls himself a shepherd in the New Testament (John 10: 11). That speaks of guidance and protection! In the Old Testament He commands us to honor Mother and Father in Exodus 20: 12. That also speaks of guidance and protection. Sheep are noticeably stupid, for the most part, first-decade kids are also. All adults grow older, but not all adults "grow up"!

So as the phases of life transpire for you in your bell shaped curve: Grow Up! Honor you parents and bring God into every part of your life. Make that last "turn" into a pearly gate, and enjoy a timeless existence with your Creator and Sustainer. It is possible that your parents will even be there.

"I Can Only Imagine"

Ecclesiastes; Final Summation #26

As Pastor Chuck finalized this amazing Book of the Scripture, I could not help but wonder, "Where have I been?" It demonstrates to me that God has a purpose in showing texts at timely points, but in His timing, not ours. I have never been a fan of reading the Bible front to back each year for just that reason. However you are better off doing that than not. I have just had a lot of experiences where I feel "led" to read passages, and I realize that God the Holy Spirit is involved.

Ecclesiastes 12 is just one of those. Verse 1 begins: "Remember your Creator in the days of your youth, before the days of trouble come". The culture which we live in today is hammering away at our faith and lifestyle. Enjoy sex, but do not get married. Take chemicals to prevent pregnancy. If that does not work, then murder your creation. Life is an accident, there is no Creator (God). Climate is subject to man's creative power and not God's handiwork. If we can just get into our DNA, then we can double life expectancy.

However Solomon came to his final conclusion to "Fear God and keep His Commandments". Is it so bad to consider a society where people do not lie, steal, hate, mess around (sexually), or cuss their Creators name continually? He then points out that "God will bring every deed into judgment… Including every hidden thing". That is enough for me my friend.

I have made more than a few trips to Europe. The most outstanding edifice in most cities is the cathedral. This is true in London, Paris, Cologne, and especially Rome. These cathedrals took literally hundreds of years to construct. They are beautiful to behold, and the indoor pillars and stained glass are magnificent. I loved the ones in Portugal. They were the centerpieces of culture and reminded people of God's creation and sustaining power in social life.

Today, our culture turns to Facebook, Twitter, and Instagram. The focus is mono-to-mono, as they say; not mono-to-Creator. We have shifted from a God-appreciation to a fellow-man-appreciation. Even

God-fearing people have been sucked in, if you will. Cathedrals by structure alone, give one a sense of "awe". Our cellphones are retained in various pockets or purses. So each and every young person has missed out on that sense of Godly awe that was apparent to all in the downtown cathedral.

Pursue life then, dear reader, without including God in the picture. The richest of society own mansions, yachts, and exclusive cars. As they die, these trinkets are left behind. Solomon calls it a life of meaninglessness (verse 8).

That sums it all up. From the wealthiest, most powerful man who ever lived? What is your focus? Do you trust your Creator? Do you believe Him? What brings meaning to your life? As Christ stated in Matthew 6: 33, "Seek first His Kingdom, and His righteousness, and all these things will be given to you as well". I came to believe these fifty years ago when I lost my business dream.

 Best thing that ever happened to me!

What is your purpose (In the immediate and the future)? Have you included God? You will be blessed!

 God guarantees it. Solomon backs Him up on it; and Jesus. And so do I!!! ☺

End Times #1 Runnin Outta Time! #27

If I was God, and boy I am not☺, then I would drop little hints about what is coming in the future. Unlike my created beings, I know what is coming! So I lace little hints/prophecies, into the older testament, and share them as the times grow near. Who cares in general? Who understood the return of Israel in 1492? Columbus was sailing West, when the eggheads of his day still thought the earth was flat (some still do in 2022; weird). The potential of Jews returning to the Promised Land was remote if even possible. On top of that, there are less than 20MM Jews today, so who really cares. God Does!!! I Do!!!

How about fewer then 20MM Jewish descendants in a population of 8 BB in 2020.

"And the Lord God of hosts, The One who builds the upper chambers in the heavens, who calls for the waters of the seas, and pours them out on the face of the earth, The Lord is His name"(Amos 9: 5, 6). "Behold the days are coming, declares the Lord, all the hills will be dissolved" (Amos 9: 13). "And in my zeal, and in my blazing wrath, I declare that on that day there will surely be a great earthquake in the land of Israel, and every wall will fall to the ground" (Ezekiel 38: 19, 20).

God has dropped His hints. In a timely manner, His plans become contemporary, and alive. God promised Abraham, and four hundred years later the Jews left Egypt for the Promised Land. God promised Daniel, and four hundred and eighty three years later, the Messiah was killed. Jesus promised His disciples, and He was killed and rose back to life in three days.

In that promise to Daniel there is still a seven year period to go. God promised when Israel is replanted (like a fig tree), when seven Christian churches have lived and died, when a world ruler takes over, and when half the world population dies or disappears, He will return as God, the Son, to rule the leftover population, and allow me to shoot par regularly☺.

But in this creation, you cannot have the beginning without the ending. Genesis 1: 1: "In the beginning, God created the heavens and the earth". 2 Peter 3: 10: "…the heavens will pass away with a roar and the elements will be destroyed with intense heat, and the earth and its works will be burned up!" Now this is the Scripture my reader, just like past prophecies, they will be fulfilled. He has tipped His hand and His plan. It is going to happen! It is just that after two thousand years of time space, the details are in place that are necessary for fulfillment.

If you are reading this, then you are probably ready, or at least prepared. I will cut to the chase: Repent! Broken any of the Ten Commandments listed in Exodus 20? Ask God to forgive you, get baptized, and go make some Christian friendships. We are running out of time you now realize. God loves His creation and He has a wonderful place set up to replace the earth for the ones who love Him back; it is called "a new Heaven and a new Earth"(Revelation 21: 1).

See you there?

End Times #2 God's Plan In Overview/Detail #28

I spent years in business hearing the adage, "make a plan". From my banker to my boss, it was always the same; "what is the plan"? If I am going to give you money, responsibility, opportunity, then what is your plan? In school the plan was an outline. Are you going to write a paper? Where is the outline and key points you will highlight and embellish? I am sure, to lay out focus, our pastor begins with an outline/plan before his sermon that sets the guidelines for what he wishes to communicate and teach.

God is not any different. In fact, you might say that He set the standard. Turn with me to Daniel 9: 24, and learn about the future. We will only discuss the outline at this point. If you want the details, then you can proceed to study for the next few years and visit Isaiah, Zachariah, the Gospels, and of course the book of Revelation. But for now, let's study the outline:

"Seventy weeks have been decreed for your people and your Holy City, to finish the transgression, to make an end to sin, to make atonement for inequity, to bring in everlasting righteousness, to seal up vision and prophecy, and to anoint the most Holy place" (Daniel 9: 24). That is God's outline for events in the future. That is what He will unfold and explain. Stick to that outline, locate the details, share it with others, and you will understand better the world within which we live today. This unfolded and explained set of details will explain the plan in detail, and the closer we get to the end, the more it clarifies. The more the outline makes sense as an avenue to, and a picture of, the future (Near and far).

Firstly, it has been ascertained, interpreted, translated, that the seventy weeks are actually seventy periods of seven years. The time period is set aside for Daniel's people; the Jews. The first sixty nine or, four hundred and eighty three years, have transpired and ended with

Christ's crucifixion, "Messiah will be cut off"; killed. That leaves one seven year period of judgment. Secondly, we see the end of the sinful experience package, rebelling against God in the transgression, and with sin, by the atonement for inequity. Christ's death, burial, and resurrection took care of those.

Thirdly than, we look forward to everlasting righteousness, seal the vision and prophecy, and anoint a most Holy place (The third Temple) (Ezekiel 40+). Sandwiched in that ending is the beautiful, glorious, powerful return of Jesus to rule and reign. What I am sharing is that packed in 1 simple verse out of sixty books, and thousands of verses, is the outline for the timed out future for humanity and in particular, the Jewish people. This was all revealed to Daniel the prophet in a visit by the Angel Gabriel. Daniel asked for a detailed explanation and God said: "Go your way Daniel, for the words are shut up and sealed until the time of the end".

Since all these items have now been opened including The New Testament, I believe that any person open to God's details will eventually understand this outline. The Jews were dispersed in 70 AD, but have returned in 1948, and the details have been rolling in. I am personally excited about the outline and the details. Excited because the time has arrived, and we are watching the details fill in the spaces. I am patient though, as I want to see more people saved. More and more, just like me! But I know God has a number in mind; in His outline. "Until the fullness of the gentiles has come in. And in this way all Israel will be saved" (Romans 11: 25).

 Enjoy your detailed search my reader. I had for fifty years. The plan is moving forward;

It is God's Perfect Plan!

End Times #3 Money & Borders #29

So I am reading a couple of emails that I receive regularly from Prophecy news and Worthy Brief today. In each of them is a short notation on digital currency in the present and the future. I then turn on the Watchman TV show hosted by Erick Stickleback, and they are on the border of Israel and Syria by the Golan Heights. The subject is Ezekiel 38 and 39, and the countries listed in that huge and described war. The players are all in place: Iran? Ethiopia? Libya? Russia? Turkey? These are the Modern names for regions that existed two thousand and five hundred years ago. I love the lead-in chapter 34 and in particular verse 27: "…and they will be secure on their land". You have to read that chapter to make sense of Israel in 2022!

As to the borders, Israel is surrounded! It is prosperous! It is wealthy! It is supported by the United States at present. God speaks of, in Ezekiel 38, pulling in these countries to attack Israel, and then causes a giant earthquake to demolish the place killing all the participants. It is so bad, that it takes seven years to clean up the bodies. Interestingly, He uses a seven year period to match the time of the Tribulation. He will throw down the mountains, and "every wall" will crumble. Read 38 and 39! I am not making this up.

If you are now getting into this, read 40+, and you will see why He levels the country. Its preparation time for the third Temple. He needs to level the place for its construction. He needs to eliminate the Dome of the Rock mosque. He details in the Jerusalem area how big the new pad will be for the Temple. God scopes out the various rooms in detail, and describes how the new Temple pad will take up space for miles. I call it the "Jesus Pad" as this will be His leadership location after He returns, and He will rule from here for thousand years (the Millennium).

As to the digital currency, we have Bitcoin, and other currencies. You can buy a new Tesla with it already! I use cash, but circulate my currency around on my computer, and pay bills each month automatically without riding my horse over to the mortgage broker to make a payment. I do not even need to holster a six shooter, but I do need a password. ☺ Revelation 13 speaks of a time people will not buy or sell without a mark/number. Tried to fly/cruise lately without a mask or vaccine? I think the world is in training.

I should lastly mention the prophecy of communication. The new Temple will exist, as best I read it, and the world sees these two guys evangelizing for three and a half years. Some beast/world leader emerges, and kills them, and the whole world sees it. I thought about that as I watched the Twin Towers crumble on TV, and especially as I watched Notre Dame Cathedral burning in real time. I do not think John knew about that ability in the future, but God did.

Have We Arrived? Is The Time Completed? Are We At The End Of A Ten Thousand Piece Puzzle?

You Have Read This. Check Out The Noted The Scriptures. Do Not Be Surprised!

I Will Not Be! ☺

End Times #5 Thief In The Night #30

I think a good place to finish the end time "Briefs" in thought and perspective for this volume, is the concept of a "thief in the night". If the Scripture has one continuum from Christ to the Apostle Paul, then it is to be expected that the prophecy is to be fulfilled, but cannot be seen on a timeline. Whether reading "The Late Great Planet Earth" of the 70's, or any of myriad books since, to my most recent rendition, "And Then the End Will Come", by Douglas Cobb, there is that continuing theme/warning. Christ will return like a thief in the night.

Christ referred to it in what is called the "Olivet Discourse" in Matthew 24. In verse 43, He states that if the "head of the household had known at what time of the night the thief was coming", the robbery could have been prevented. Paul repeats the warning in 1 Thessalonians 5: 2 when he equates Christ's first return happening "like a thief in the night". When we refer back to Matthew 24 again, we read about Noah's day in verses 37-39.

In Noah's day they just kept on living life, with no thought to where the path of life led. Crazy Noah was building this huge ship out in the desert for one hundred and twenty years. There was not any noticeable water that would float this behemoth vessel, as he, and hundreds of workers, labored to finish a ship that covered two football fields in size. At the same time Noah was collecting animals from around his world, and grew them and corralled them for the trip. I am sure when the day came, there was a huge assemblage to watch as the giant gangplank was lifted by God and it slammed shut against the Ark.

Think back with me! One hundred and fifteen years ago, my father and mother were born. They actually rode horses, and they also worked on their farms. In their 20's, they lived in the roaring 20's. Dad's family owned a Stutz Bearcat automobile. That is pretty fancy dear reader. They both lived through two World Wars and saw men walk on the moon. So do not sell Noah (and God) short. Noah changed transportation in his day, and God changed the weather. Be careful with climate change. What has happened to us in one hundred and fifteen years?

The Ark then was a symbol for the earth dwellers to see and potentially prepare for God's judgment on lifestyles and Godlessness. Eight people came through! Are we in those days again? More than eighty percent of the world's population is oblivious to what is going on. We crazy Noahs of our day are warning the masses that God is again ready to judge our world for sin, and unbelief. Any "day" now, the door will slam shut, and the rain will fall and our friends and relatives, and co-workers, and neighbors might say, "Hey, what is that stuff falling out of the sky"? Get It?

Do not get caught by surprise my friend. Accept my umbrella! Better yet, come on board. Set up surveillance. Get motion detectors. Be ready for the thief. The Spiritual solution is to read the Bible and reach out to your Creator. Check out His Son, and heed His advice on lifeboat maneuvers. As in Noah's days, "they were eating and drinking; they were marrying and giving in marriage". Do not rise to discover and that everything you hold dear in this world was taken last night by the thief you did not plan and prepare for.

Wake Up!

End Times Russia Hooked? Is Prophecy Being Fulfilled Today? #31

As I create this particular one Page Brief, the newscasts are perilous. A country called Ukraine is being overrun by a country called Russia. It makes no sense at all, as the entire world is upset, leading to financial markets closing down against Russia, along with trading and travel. One has to scratch their head as to any reason one could think why Russia would do this. My grandkids might discuss it at the local pub or friendly party with friends. But, is it a "God" thing?

In Ezekiel 36, the return scenario of Israel begins. By the 3eighth chapter, we are well into the prophetic story. Israel returns (1948), and the world gathers around to object. Israel re-forms, as you see, right in the middle of all the Arabs, and Muslims. Verse 3 calls out the participants. Verse 4 reads God putting "hooks" in the jaws of these countries to advance toward Israel (pictured on Genesis 10 of my ESV Bible). Let's develop this picture and check out the map in 2022. Are we on the brink of the fulfilled prophecy?

So the Bible delineates the countries and processes that work out during the end times. But what would attract the Northern country (Russia) to Ukraine today? This country is loaded with natural resources like Uranium and titanium for example. They produce up to 15% of the world's exports for wheat and corn. If Russia gains back this territory, Putin and his oligarch buddies are set in this life. Is not that the driving force? Ask Gates, Bezos, or Musk!

Back to the Bible!

These northern countries will be drawn down (hooked) to invade, and destroy Israel. Ukraine is on the border of Turkey (Asia Minor). God said He will "put hooks" in the mouths of these countries listed from Gog (Russia?), down through Turkey and Syria to rule the world and the oil industry, in my opinion. I believe personally, that the Russian move with three-fourth of their army makes little sense, unless the time has arrived, and Ukraine makes sense in the present to Russia (they are hooked). However, God really gets mad☹, creates an earthquake (verse 19), and not only wipes out the armies, but levels every hill and wall in Israel. That is what it reads!

Read It Yourself! Ezekiel 38, 39

Yes I believe that we have arrived. We do need one another event to take place that is referred to as "the rapture". That is for another "Brief".

Ezekiel also notes these events will create such a mess that it will take seven years to clean it up (and Russia will wish that they have stayed at home and not listened to Putin)! Now this was written two thousand and five hundred years ago, and it is fun to watch it unfolded. Of course, I do not live in Ukraine or Israel. But when you are on the winning team, then it is fun to play in the Super Bowl.

So it is a God thing. Is it not always? You are just not aware of it. As you grow (mature) in your faith, and study a lot then you become more sensitive to God working the program personally. I believe that we might be in the most exciting time even, excluding Jesus Christ's time on earth. As Jesus told His disciples: "Enjoy the fishing trip!" (John 21).

But Go Fishing, Will You?

End Times The 70 Week Period Of Time # 32

Probably one of the main time periods of what is called "the end times" is a seven-year period called the "Tribulation Period". It is covered in the Book of Revelation chapters 6-19. To get to the point, non-believers in the God of Creation, and His Son, and the Holy Spirit, will go through a seven-year period of judgment, with about half of them dying and the other half wishing they were dead. At the end of this, God's adversary (Satan) will be locked up for a thousand years, and Christ will return.

The key for me is that this period is introduced in Daniel 9, as one of sixty nine such periods taking place ending with the 70th. Around the turn of the 20th century (1900) Sir Robert Anderson painstakingly worked out the dates in Daniel's (God's) chapter 9 prophecy. From a proclamation for the Jews to return to Israel, until the Messiah is killed, takes up the first sixty nine weeks or four hundred and eighty three years. That then left one period of seven years to fulfill the seventy year totality. "Seventy weeks are decreed for "your" people" (Daniel 9: 24). Not all people, or other people, or people of faith, But "your" people. Daniel's people were the Jewish people.

When seen in this light, I believe it explains, in part, why Christians do not feel the seven year tribulation is meant for them. Non-Christians do not even know about it. This is a final period of time when God will bring final judgment to the world's people and system that rails against Him and His glory. In this process of time He will also purify His people and prove His covenant. He will lead the campaign with one hundred and forty four thousand born-again Jews to proclaim His reality to the world.

Prophecy absolutely clarifies as it is fulfilled. To me it seems to clarify as the time approaches. A great deal has happened in my lifetime to verify that we are in the "end times"; near the time when Christ will return (Just as when He left, Acts 1). Christ gave out some of the details in Matthew 24. Some of the keys are a system of not buying or selling without I.D. Another would be 2 witnesses being seen around the world as they are killed and resurrected. These events are now possible, but they were not when John transcribed the Revelation.

That leaves us with one key event; the rebirth of Israel. That would be like the Indians retaking Manhattan, if you ask me. Why do not you ask the Arabs? Read the prophecy in Ezekiel 36-39. It is a bit like reading the New York Times. It is happening! Now! Pastor Daryl shared the fulfilled prophecy of Christ's birth this evening, working off of Micah 5: 1-5. It happened. But then Christ allowed 30 years to pass before He was baptized and exercised His ministry. Are we in that time period? We do not know the day, but we do know the times. Are you ready?

Have we arrived? China, Russia (GOG?), Iran (Persia?) all have nukes. Israel is right in the middle of its enemies listed in Ezekiel 38. America seems hell bent on destruction from within: Trillions in debt, murdering the unborn, throwing out the Ten Commandments. Need I go on? I Thessalonians calls for the removal of all believers alive and dead, at some point. It makes, beyond, perfect sense that this would happen prior to God punishing the World system and its followers, and before the purification of "Daniel's people".

So there you have it, my reader, there was a time for the Jews in Egypt, in the desert, in Babylon, and now in the Tribulation. Praise the God that I got saved when the covenant people of God were dispersed for their sin. I take no pleasure in the Jewish periods of separation and punishment.

But I Take Great Pleasure In My Salvation And Attendant Forgiveness! ☺

All aboard. It is the seventy week express and it is leaving the station abruptly. Do not miss the train!

End Times 2 Minute Warning New Year's #33

All football fans know that many, if not most games, are won in the fourth quarter. Lombardi of Green Bay Packer fame said more points were scored in the last two minutes of the first and second half of each game than any other time of the game.

I propose that we are in the last 2 minutes of this age, and we now know what kind of shape we are in. Do we suck it up and play harder? Or do we cave from fatigue? Do we pale in the security of our riches, having all physical and security needs afforded? Or do we recognize our depravity and the need to dig in defensively, or pound forth offensively? Have you been worn down by illness, Pandemic, Ukraine, or old age?

For those who are aware, we are in the most exciting period of written history. All history exists around the events of Creation in Genesis to the re-Creation of Heaven at the end of the Apocalypse. We have been chosen to exist, period, and at this time, as an opportunity. This is no time to be tired. The end indeed, has to be near. I will share another brief focusing on last/latter days.

Therefore, having this knowledge and incentive, work harder (fellowship and share salvation) (toss a bunch of seeds) (Mark 4, Matthew 13), work all the smarter (study the Scriptures, either alone or in fellowship), and ask God to have His Spirit lead you in living, as Christ set the example (be born-again and not religious).

Do not be bothered if you falter in your actions (sin/penalty), or not complete the pass (share the Gospel in spite of rejection), or find yourself running around to avoid tackles (being out of Fellowship).

Press on for the prize and score (touchdown/field goal), and win the game (meet Christ and loved ones in heaven). You can always rest when the game is over, and appreciate you were a part of the winning program 😊

End Times Latter/Last Days #34

I have been led to read the Minor Prophets of late. I liken it to finishing a thousand piece puzzle. It has been a long trip through Genesis, Exodus, Psalms, Ecclesiastes, Daniel, Zechariah, Malachi, Matthew, Mark, Luke, John, Romans, Ephesians, and Revelation, with multiple stops in between. In my travelling days, I reached every physical State in the union, all but 3 Capitals, the Caribbean, Europe (1 Dozen times), China, and Israel. Travelling the free world, and perusing the Scriptures, has been a Joyride!

The Bible then, is God's trip through and with His creation. It has a beginning (Genesis 1), and an ending (2 Peter 3 10). The Bible does not teach evolution going back billions of years, nor does it picture the earth lasting another billion years. Here today, gone tomorrow! We are on a clock my friend. God speaks of "His" people and "His" return to work with them, in the near future. In Hosea 3: 4 & 5, He spells it out as He proclaims: "the children of Israel shall return and seek the Lord their God, and David their King, and they shall come in fear to the Lord and to His goodness, In The Latter Days".

In Micah 4: 1 God says, "It shall come to pass in the latter days". He then goes on to say that the House of the Lord will be established and people will flow to it. Then He says that the Word of the Lord will flow out of Jerusalem. Lastly, during that time, nation shall not lift sword against nation. Has that happened yet in history? I think the puzzle has a few pieces left to go.

Isaiah 2: 2 states: "It shall come to pass in the "latter days". It goes on to say: "the mountain of the House of the Lord… and many people's shall come and say: Come let us go up to the mountain of the Lord… that He may teach us His ways". I believe this spoke of the Millennium-year period.

Daniel was denied the privilege of prophetic understanding at the end of his ministry. He was given that same prognostication concerning the "End Of Days" being told the antichrist must come and sit in the

Temple and the sacrifices ended. Again, this has not yet happened. As a matter of fact, we can go to Matthew 24: 15: "when you see the Abomination of Desolation spoken of by the Prophet Daniel, standing in the Holy Place", and down through verse 31, we see the latter day's scenario. This is Christ's rendition and it has not yet happened. The Tribulation takes place, and Christ returns. Christ's admonition: "Get Outta Town".

We have covered it now in the Old and New. God has a plan, and has laid it out. So take Christ's advice:

Get Outta Town

End Times The Rapture #35

To every born-again Bible student Christian in 2022, this event is one of the most significant upcoming things to happen in modern history. Firstly, it has not happened. Secondly, the event is covered in 1 Thessalonians 4: 16 and 17; "Christ Himself will descend from heaven with a shout" (come up here). We will meet in the air. Thirdly, after it happens, the antichrist will take a seat in the third Temple. That has not happened either. We therefore have a prophesied event which must take place in the (near) future, when all Christians on earth at that point will be called by our Lord to meet Him "in the air". His actual second coming (to Earth) is covered in Zachariah 14 when His feet touch the ground (Mount of Olives). This Rapture event is seven years earlier and He does not touch the earth.

So the big issue for some is exactly when this event takes place. I find it easy to surmise while some claim it to be a different time. Firstly, in Daniel 9: 24 God prophesizes through Daniel "Seventy weeks have been decreed for "your" people; not all people! Daniel's people were the Jewish people. We have studied and learned these predicted times are defined in years, and not in actual weeks. That is how God keeps things mysterious for non-believers as Christ did with His parables.

Forty nine of the weeks/years have already passed. They predicted Christ's death to the year/day (?). And there are seven years (one week) to go. The timing is perfect and set up for those of the Jewish lineage. God needs no cooperation anymore then what He would have needed with Abraham for His covenant back in Genesis 15. So this last period of seven years then is only for the Jewish people when it occurs. It all manifests with the re-emergence of Israel (Ezekiel 39: 25-29). Our parents witnessed the event in 1948. That was akin to the Indians of New York taking back Manhattan Island in 1948.

So what more logical/Scriptural time would be appropriate to remove Christians from the face of the earth, then when the last person to be saved was added. "Until the fullness of the gentiles has come in"

(Romans 11: 25). You do not think God has a number? No comment! At that time the judgment of the world can begin. My judgment, along with my fellow believers, was handled on the Cross by my Savior's sacrifice for me, and I will not diminish the sacrifice of that event, for anything. The Book of Revelation covers the church age in chapters 2 and 3, and the church is not mentioned on earth again in chapters 4-21.

So I excitedly look forward to this upcoming taking away of all Christian believers, before this terrible time of earthly judgment. This position is commonly known in Christian eschatological studies as "pre-tribulation". Extended; that connotes a pre-Tribulation Rapture. Christians are not meant to be judged again, as Christ "Did It All" at Cavalry.

Lastly one might ask: "where are the believers who were raptured than"? Look closely at chapters 4 and 5 of Revelation and you will see. Billions of believers will be celebrating, praising, worshipping, and humbled before the throne of God and our Creator. When that most magnificent worship service of all time concludes, we will join Christ to return and finish His work on earth, Revelation 19: 11-14.

Get ready to ride!

Equipping The Saints #36

I learned my lesson at age fifteen as I experienced my first football game. I am so old, we did not have facemasks to protect us on our helmets. As the second screen center that could not do one push up, the coach put me in and said "grit your teeth at him Shafer". I did, and the defensive lineman said, "Oh, you think you are tough huh"? He then kneaded me in the face, and I wanted to run home for mother's comfort. I Was Not Equipped!

Fast forward to junior year, and I grew. I lettered the next six years through college and started as a high school senior and then my last two years in college. In college my workout included sixty pushups and two hundred sit-ups for a warm-up, and my weight workout was with two hundred lbs. I Was Equipped!

I started learning about my faith in high school and college, if people asked, I was a Christian. Toward my late 20's, I opened a class for my friend Terry like an announcer (or comic, if you will), and enjoyed it immensely. I was not equipped! I later taught that same class which grew to two hundred, mostly, young couples. I used a workbook by Stuart Briscoe, a commentary by William Barclay, and listened to tapes by a young John MacArthur. I taught the book about Joy; Philippians, and I Was Equipped!

In the letter to the Ephesians 4: 11, we read the purpose for preaching and teaching is to equip the saints. I read what the Apostles and Prophets had to say. I heard many times what Billy Graham had to say, as an Evangelist, and asked Jesus to forgive and save me at age ten or eleven. But in verse 11, Paul adds Pastors and Teachers "for the equipping of the Saints for the work of service, to the building up of the Body of Christ". He did not told us to hire pastors to get all the work done! I have experienced various pastors over the years, and the best, of course, were the ones who understood this concept of training and delegation.

In high school we won three games in two years. In college, we only lost three games in 4 years. Guess where I had the better coach. I often wondered why someone would even be bothered practicing if they were on the third string. I guess it was for the athletic love for the game. I guess that explains church attendance.

When I was a second stringer, I really wanted to be on the first string. But, I needed to train, and Get Equipped. It was a tough road as I was growing. My business career path was crumbling from age twenty five to forty. But during that time, my Spiritual life was growing as I was Getting Equipped For The Work Of The Ministry. After age forty, both my business career, and my Spiritual journey accelerated successfully. I Was Equipped!

There are good coaches and bad coaches. There are great preachers/teachers, and not so great. Move around until you find one/some that Equip You For The Work. And then Do It!

There is no better service in this life than sharing God's creation, His love for His creation, and His Son Jesus Christ who facilitated His creation.

Now, Get To Work!!! ☺

Eternal Life #37

I think this is the greatest message of The Scripture that I have learned! I have run into, shared, discussed, and argued about what this stupid life is all about. When I say stupid, let me digress☺. People who have succeeded beyond monetary average spend time talking about second cars, second homes, cruises, vacations to remote countries, and what they will leave to their children. If you truly consider it, then it is a foolish to live three score and ten, only to become a pile of dirt, and leave any amassed wealth to your offspring for more earthly enjoyment.

The Bible takes it up a step, and reveals life as going beyond this existence, if you have studied it. Elijah proved something was ongoing when he left in a cloud (2 Kings 2: 11, 12). I look forward to my "Chariot Of Fire" someday. The now famous John 3: 16 promises eternal life to those who believe and trust in Jesus. A key to that verse is "shall not parish". That is the big secret/mystery, that life is eternal.

This thought is covered back in the Old Testament book of Daniel 12: 2. It acknowledges that people "sleep in the dust" (Die), but it then speaks of a resurrection. This is covered in part at 1 Thessalonians 4: 16 for believers. It is then again covered in Revelation 20: 11-15. So I guess death is not permanent, which means that life is. I try to share that with my friends who believe that this life is the whole package/game, but it seldom gets through. I will still keep sharing!

So how did Christ describe it? "Now this is eternal life; that they may know you, the only true God and Jesus Christ, whom you have sent" (John 17: 3). Christ's point in prayer to His/our Father is that knowing them is eternal life. Once you have traversed that point of knowledge; you are in. From someone who has spent his whole existence in a time-zone, I am very excited. The promise of eternal life and all the accompanying benefits is really exciting. Moving into that phase without faith in our Creator is not possible.

73

So eternal life, is knowing Him. "I want to know Christ and the power of His Resurrection" (Philippians 3: 10). Do you want to live forever with your Creator?

Get To Know Him! ☺

Eternal Life Secured #38

As Pastor Kyle focused on 1 Peter last week, and in particular: 1 Peter 1: 3, 4, one can read about the promise of faith in our Creator and the sacrifice of God, the Son, Jesus Christ. Based on God's mercy, and the resultant New Birth, and due to Christ's resurrection, we are promised to never perish in our Heavenly abode as we look forward. Now that is something to be excited about!

This guy (Peter the Apostle) had a major turnaround; from fisherman to theologian. Seminary Doctorates study his writings, preach his writings, and work at living his writings. Of course, born-again believers realize that he was inspired by the Holy Spirit (2 Timothy 3: 16). It is just amazing to me that someone of Peter's pedigree could be used by God to propagate the Gospels at this level. Could that be true in 2022? Hmmmmm!

He speaks here of a "Living Hope", not a dead one, not one in the past, but one in the present and future. He speaks of, and repeats what John spoke of in the third Chapter of His gospel that Pastor Jon just covered in his preachments. The Bible speaks to those of us who were born and are alive in the flesh (humans). As Jesus said to Nicodemus, "you must be born again"! So getting to heaven is that critical reward for those who accept the eternity of existence in this life. As one translation says, it is "imperishable, undefiled, and unfading" (verse 4).

So get with the program, dear reader. You must figure out if you have not already, what it means to be born again. Millions if not billions already have. Billions already have not! Read these verses from Peter multiple times until you Get It! It is a promise from God, through Peter that you can live forever with our Savior in Heaven. Christ proved that death is not permanent when He resurrected, and walked around for forty days eating, drinking, and breathing with His disciples; on earth! Then He shot up into the clouds like a rocket ship and disappeared for the present. But He Did Promise To Return!

For me, I love the part where Peter notes that we have an inheritance coming: Kept In Heave. Have you read the last two chapters of the Bible in Revelations? Wow, what a trip. Fresh water, fresh fruit, no death! No sadness, no tears, no changing the light bulbs, or gassing up. What a place to spend eternity. I have added a couple of more things, but not in print. So get your eternal life secured, if you have not already. I will meet you at the heavenly golf course, where we can shoot a few birdies!

Fooooorrrreeee

Faith And Loyalty #39

My Rabbi Dave taught a lesson last week and focused on Faith and Loyalty as two of the main attributes of a God-created human being. As one peruses the Scriptures then, you focus on people such as Abraham, Noah, Job, David, Daniel, John the Baptist, and Paul, just to name a few. You cannot exemplify faith and loyalty to God, our Creator, and Christ, our sustainer, and the Holy Spirit, our influencer, and not mention these men of the Bible. We also cannot leave out the great ladies from Ruth, Esther, and Deborah, to Elizabeth, to the greatest of all women, in my opinion, Mary, who was picked to be the earthly mother of Jesus.

"Faith" is defined as "complete trust or confidence in someone or something".

"Loyalty" is defined as "a strong feeling of support or allegiance".

Can you mention these traits, and not think of the ones listed above. That is what the Bible is all about. That is for what it was written in part. It lists a detailed history of life in the past and who lived it then. Forget the past, and you will miss the purpose for the present, and the prospects for the future. We are facing that disaster in the present in our country today. Our forefathers wanted to be free and they wrote and signed the "Declaration of Independence".

The key message they sought to convey, based on in whom their faith rested, was that we were granted "by our Creator, life, liberty, and the pursuit of happiness". Sounds like Ecclesiastes to me! I wish the schools would get back to teaching these truths again. I am afraid the teachers of today cannot pass on what they have not been taught themselves. As Paul relayed in Romans 10: 15 "How beautiful are the feet of those who bring glad tidings of good things", as He quoted Isaiah 52: 7.

Isaiah 52: 7: "How lovely on the mountains are the feet of him who brings good news, who announces peace, and brings good news of happiness, who announces salvation, and says to Zion, 'your Lord reigns'!" All the average student, at ASU, needs do, is cast his or her net across Mill Ave, in Tempe, break loose from the swarm, and hear the "good news" being taught out of the bestselling book in the history of mankind. This book was once taught in public school, and was the foundational primmer at Harvard, Yale, and Princeton. Now that society has thrown out the Ten Commandments, How is It Going?

A guy came along in the 1400's, named Martin Luther. His favorite verse was (Romans 1: 17) "But the righteous man shall live by faith" (Habakkuk 2: 4). So if you wish to be a "good" person, the issue is your faith. Not the level of your faith, but the "object" of your faith. Many, over the ages of history (known past events in time) have lost their lives over the objects of their faith. They were not great people of God as listed above, but they were nonetheless saved by Grace (Ephesians 2: 8, 9). In more recent times, I think of Martin Luther, and Martin Luther King, or William Wilberforce, or George Washington, or others who made great sacrifices based on the objects of their faith and loyalty.

Got Anyone Else In Mind? Is One The Face In The Mirror?

Ask Today: Whom Will I Serve!

To Whom Will I Extend My Faith And My Loyalty?

You Might Be More Important Then You Realize ☺

Faith/Demonstrated #40

I get tired by people who constantly speak of the faith they have, or had, but little is seen in the demonstration. I refuse to attack anyone as I have too many of my own sins or shortcomings on the way to criticizing others. There are some denominations more critical than others, and I believe we could all use a large slice of humble pie with our regular meals and fellowship. Preach the Gospel; criticize others later.

I heard a great message the other day from a female teacher/preacher. She noted that everyone has muscles, but only the ones who exercise them, show them. I understood that in college when weightlifting was a continual habit in readying me for football. I worked out with 200's, and had sixteen inch biceps. I was the long-snapper and it was useful. Now seven decades later, I use 10 weights with increased repetitions. In either case, the old dormant muscles expand and are noticed.

Do you believe? Exercise your muscle! Go to church! Join a fellowship and join a small share group or Bible study. Help out in your fellowship from fixing the facilities up, teaching, or helping with the children. Join a men's or women's group and share and grow.

Exercise And Grow Those Faith Muscles!

I work out at the local workout gym center. Some guys, and a few gals, are in spectacular shape. To yell at them to do more would be like preaching to the Choir. They are there and exercising! It is just like the local church. Most strong Christians are there and they are exercising. Do you have a friend or relative that shows no muscle in the faith? They are not working out, are they? They do not show up, they give what is left over, and they cannot fill their left hand with Christian friends.

I think the analogy is spectacular. Get to work. Are there any hidden muscles in the born-again world? Have you read or re-read the parable of the talents? (Matthew 25: 14-30). Have you read that last verse? He threw the "worthless" servant into the outer darkness. If you wish to study the good side of things, then read verses 31-40. The guidelines for service are there; the balance of the chapter deals with the fate of those not exercising.

It is a life and death game my friend. If you have never worked out with weights, then you might not understand. It is hard, it takes determination, and it takes Faith! If you are not "working out" you might not have the Faith. "Choose This Day" (Joshua 24: 15). But by all means:

Start Exercising

Fasting #41

Fasting is the process of not ingesting food and nutrition. It can also be isolated to limit the consumption of processed sugar, as I am presently doing. My goal is to focus on the next twenty days, as I have already passed the first twenty. I have exercised low carbohydrate diets in the past, and they can be painful. Eliminating processed sugar is much easier. The average US Citizen consumes 150's of sugar each year. My guidebook is "The 40-Day Sugar Fast" by Wendy Speake.

Back to the Bible!

On the way to Galilee from Jerusalem the disciples said to Jesus: "Rabbi, eat" (John 4: 31). Jesus had fasted earlier when He spent forty days in the wilderness (Luke 4: 2). Moses fasted for forty days when receiving the Ten Commandments, twice! (Exodus 34: 28). Elijah also fasted for forty days later, after receiving heavenly food (1 Kings 19: 8). So my little exercise of forty days without processed sugar is nothing.

Let me share another perspective. Potato chips do not have any sugar. I mention that because in this particular fast one can give up sugar, and not give up carbohydrates. I have done the low carb diet, and it, as I said above, can be painful. After many different tries in life, it is also boring. The reality of high protein and low carbohydrates is dramatic weight reduction, if necessary. So what is your focus? Is it the body, or the Spirit; or both?

So let's go back to John 4. What was Christ talking about? "My food is to do the will of Him who sent Me, and to accomplish His work" (John 4: 34). I learned here that my mouth and God's work are diametrically opposed! I have learned that modern suburban eating and drinking run in opposition to serving "In The Spirit". So much for church pot lucks. ☹ When it was time for Moses, Elijah, and Jesus to go to work, they fasted. We turn to mouth entertainment.

There is a significant argument amongst Christians as to the power of one's free will. The Bible seems, if not does, eliminate that as to salvation (Ephesians 2: 8, 9). I am not sure, to be sure, but if so, I am grateful and thankful. Please do not say this to the Baptists you know, or at least be graciously kind. I do not think it is a hill to die on, if one believes and trusts the Gospel. But I do see the free will, in what we eat/ingest. Does it taste good, or is it healthy, or is it too much? How does your will lead you?

You will probably react as the disciples did. Your Dad said to "eat your meat". Your Mom said to "eat your vegetables". They both said to "clean your plate". My father would then remind me of all the starving children in China, at that time. Christ, as you saw from the above verses, was focused on God's Word, and not God's food. His harvest was focused on the conversion of people, not grain. Is Yours?

Try fasting (denial) for a day from eating, drinking, smoking, and fighting or… then turn to food. You just do not! You will realize how dependent you are on self-sustenance. Your body, mind, but not your Spirit (being saved) will fight you tooth and nail. Just refocus from jelly beans to Jesus.

It Is Harder, But It Is A Lot Better High!

Forgiveness/Forgiven #42

The essence of the Christian faith is forgiveness. In the prayer that Christ taught us, we are asking our Creator (Genesis 1: 1). to forgive our sins as we forgive those who sin against us (Matthew 6: 12). This set of actions is both linear and circular. Anyone so blessed that has awareness, wants to be forgiven. Forgiving others, however, seems a bit more difficult.

Have you been wronged by a neighbor or business associate? "Judge Judy" makes millions on TV off of these conflicts. Have you been seemingly or actually wronged by a spouse? Divorce is rampant today, and leads to heartache, bankruptcy, and the desolation of the family structure. Has there been any time in the history of mankind that countries are not warring against one another? Would that be an issue, if people were forgiving "one another" (Ephesians 4: 32)?

Is this really a chicken and egg scenario? What comes first, if anything? I propose that one cannot forgive, who has not been forgiven. As our society is crumbling before our eyes, the hallmark of existence stands out as condemnation, and competition. We condemn one another, as we compete. We pick sides or teams, and cheer on to the death, as the Romans did in the Empire. As I watch and enjoy the Super Bowl, the NBA playoffs, or the Stanley Cup, I am surprised they do not play to the death! God knows that the audience would be pleasured.

But that is what our wars are about. In this day and age, look up Putin, or Xi Jinping, or the Ayatollahs. In my lifetime, look up Hitler or Stalin, or the Emperor of Japan. In World War two, we saw the death of over sixty million souls. The blood flowed for a lack of forgiveness. In ancient history, the blood flowed in Israel, Egypt, Assyria, and elsewhere. In the future, the blood will flow again as we face into the great Tribulation (Revelation 14: 20).

So I guess this "sin nature" stuff has some reality. All sin is, is the antithesis of who God, our Creator is. God is Love! (1John 4: 8)

Whoever does not Love, does not know God. I have lately focused on conflicts as the competition between the "God-Fearing", and the "Godless"! Can you love your Creator and hate your neighbor, or your spouse, or your offspring? I think not, and the Scripture leads us elsewhere.

So I implore you today, appropriate the Love of our God and Creator. Get forgiven, if you have not as of yet. And then and now:

Forgive As You Have Been Forgiven!

Free Will To… #43

I heard a message the other week on being Born-Again. That is what Christ said to Nicodemus the Pharisee in John 3, had to happen so he could "see" the Kingdom of Heaven. I have just been studying the Kingdoms of this earth in Daniel, and I am now really looking forward to God's Kingdom in heaven as opposed to the one's here from Nebuchadnezzar to Putin. I have never been as excited as now, and share the Apostle Paul's vision: "For to me, to live is Christ, and to die is gain"!

My problem is that I constantly think about and act out sin. I would like to think, and I do feel, that I sin less than in the past, but I am not sure that I could bank that profit compared to living a perfect life or thought process. I have lusted, lied, swore, felt greedy, and cussed. I might as well confess, if for no other reason than to make you feel better knowing that you are not the only one. ☺

I do not believe that free will gets us in based on Ephesians 2: 8, 9. Even Romans 3: 11 states: "There is none who seeks for God". So God opens our heart/eyes, but some kind of free will cuts in at that point.

Read Colossians 3: 1-15: "Set your mind on the things above and not on the things that are on earth" (verse 2). It seems that we have a choice as a result of salvation, after we are blessed with being chosen. "Consider the members of your earthly body as dead to immorality, impurity, passion, evil desire, and greed…". There is a choice? I think that is where the free will steps in. "But now you also, put them all aside: anger, wrath, malice, slander, and abusive speech from your mouth" (verse 8).

"And so as those who have been chosen" (verse 12), do all the good things. This fits in well with Romans 7 where he admits to the constant conflict in life after salvation takes place in one's life. He ends this treatise with "let the peace of Christ rule in your hearts" (verse 15). It is my position after fifty years of study and practice that the concept of free will takes place after one is born again. We get a choice to do what God wants us to, because He has joined with us and has imputed <u>His</u> thoughts in us.

If we all grew to the point where we practiced verses 12-13, we would be too busy forgiving with our free wills than to be sinning! This chapter 3 in the letter to the church in Colossi spells it out. If you are saved, then you have a daily choice. Your "free will" can take you one way or the other. Or as that great theologian Yogi Berra once said:

"When you reach a fork in the road, take it!"

From Womb To Tomb God Knows #44

One of the biggest questions in life is whether God is the Creator of life or some distant Deity that is unknowable, and unreachable. The Bible is explicit about those questions and starts right out at the beginning with "In the Beginning". Today we will refer to Psalm 139. At some time in our growth as a born-again Christian, we learn that the Bible (The Scripture) is God's Word (2 Timothy 3: 16). He authored the entirety of the 66 books, and had it written in its entirety by His noted Prophets and Disciples.

Psalm 139 is so written, and reveals information in an easily read one-chapter form. It covers our individual creation, His attention to the details in our life, and the believer's destiny. It is a truly amazing documentary worth even memorizing. Let's begin at the beginning:

"You formed my inward parts, you knitted me together in my mother's womb. My frame was not hidden from You, when I was being made in secret" (verse 13-15). If your newly conceived baby is an inconvenience, then I would not consider abortion as an option. Would you consider it an option to extricate God's creation? If you do not know God the Creator, then you might consider this tragedy against creation. But if you do know Him, it is not an option!

Are you worried about your life's path? "You know when I sit down and rise up…You search out my path and my lying down…even before a word is on my tongue…You know it altogether" (verse 2-4) (a step ahead of Alexis). According to The Scripture, God seems to be on top of all the details. If you watch TV today, then you can see cameras, and microphones, and identity devices, and face recognition, and Alexis in people's homes, that can record and hear and answer anything done or said. Do not believe it? Google It! ☺

"And lead me in the way everlasting" (verse 24). How is that for a final verse? He claims our creation. He claims our life process, and

He lastly claims our "everlasting existence". I have been following a young man named Charlie Kirk of recent. He is a young born-again Christian who is active in conservative politics. He has jumped into K-12 education due to the Godless takeover of education in our country. Check out "Turning Point TP USA". We now have to fight for the educational process as we look forward to the everlasting.

After decades of study, and rubber meets the road experience, I can read Psalm 139, and appreciate the God of creation, process, and eternity. The veracity of this chapter gives proof of God's interest and investment in each of our lives. So many times I have tried to squeeze God into "my" box. Modern technology has proven the limitless potential of the Creator God who in His uninhibited stature can know me and guide me, and hold me in Love and graciousness. I sincerely look forward to the everlasting segment at my ripe old age, and am reminded however that:

To Live Is Christ!

Giving #1 #45

The whole essence of Christianity is in the giving and not the taking. The whole essence of our fallen natures since Adam and Eve is in the taking and not the giving. The contrast is spelled out in the life of Christ versus the life of the religious leaders that He faced during His earthly sojourn. John 1-3 pretty much capsulated Christ's life and purpose. John further writes his three Epistles toward the end of the New Testament to speak of God the Son's role in the Spirit of Love and giving.

Want to know about your (UN) born-again nature? My Rabbi suggests we read Matthew 23. In that chapter, Christ castigates/attacks the Scribes and the Pharisees as a group of phonies and hypocrites seeking praise and adoration based on their vocation and roles at the Temple. Christ visits the Temple twice, as I understand, to uproot the dishonest and corrupt money changers that were allowed in there by the Pharisaical management team. It makes me think of Washington D.C., and get mildly sympathetic for January sixth of last year even though I abhor what took place.

So what was the New Testament version for giving? Nowhere does it give any limited figure or percentage as a minimum. Christ Himself took note of a widow whom He observed, and suggested it was not the amount, but the attitude (Mark 12: 43-44). "This poor widow put in more than all the contributors to the treasury; for they all put in out of their surplus. But she, out of her poverty, put in all she owned, all she had to live on". Have you given all you own lately??? I have not!

God does not ask that of us materially, but He does spiritually. It is somewhere between ten percent by the phonies, and a hundred percent by the widow. Always remember, I/you can print a check, but God can print a galaxy!!!

Some guidelines will get us through: "Give and it will be given to you" (Luke 6: 38), "freely you received, freely give" (Matthew 10: 8), "It is more blessed to give then to receive" (Acts 20: 35).

Giving is Cathartic! You can read Giving #2 for the explanation. The key in this whole process is to be the Sea of Galilee, and not the Dead Sea. These two great lakes of Israel and Jordan, of all that is living, and all that is dead, are connected in process by the Jordan River. One end is alive, fresh, and giving. The other is taking, settling, and dead.

So let's check attitudes today. Are we cringing (and I have) over ten dollars in the offering plate, and then spending twenty dollars on lunch? How much is it for a movie or a ball game? How much is it to spread the good news, that got me saved, or to help the poor and needy out of my blessing from my Creator (Ezekiel 16: 49, 50)?

I have got faith in you. I have hope for you. Let's go share our blessings while we have time! ☺

Giving #2 Cathartic Giving #46

I have shared for months with my pastor/counselor how cathartic an exercise writing these "Briefs" has been personally. "Get it off your chest"! Actually, I was not thinking of my chest, but rather my bladder. Any healthy or unhealthy octogenarian knows about catheters. They are used to drain bodily fluids that would otherwise be retained. The result is relieving for sure, but sometimes painful in process.

At some time in my last decade, I had a personal roto-rooter job done which ended blockage, frequency, and some pain! Have you ever had that mentally? It is a multi-billion dollar industry. We have a full time, fully scheduled pastor at our church to listen to the drainage. My hope is that this cathartic experience on my part will help others who suffer from limited relief at present.

The question is how do I personally become cathartic or at least initiate cathartic activities? The writer of Hebrews says "And do not forget to do good and to share with others for with such sacrifices, God is pleased" (Hebrews 13: 16). As opinions ring, however, we say: "different strokes for different folks". What is cathartic for me may not be for thee!

To help explain how people are different, I am an outgoing, sports-minded, ex-National Sales Manager. My wife is not. My cathartic experiences are much different than hers. She sews sachet bags, or sends flowers, or picks cards. You are reading my expressions in the multiples in these written "Briefs". They just keep coming! She does however, have a basketful of sachet bags. I think where couples exasperate one another is at that point, mutual catharses no longer gain expression physically. At the same time, "let's sit down and talk this one out" no longer works either.

So what is your cathartic expression? It must flow outward for someone else. Remember when the woman in the crowd touched the garment that Jesus was wearing? "If I only touch His cloak, I will be healed" (Matthew 9: 20, 21). Wow did she have the faith? Christ felt that touch and responded "your faith has healed you". Oh that we had that activated faith in our lives today! The thing is to me that Christ was a totally giving persona, if only the people around Him would seek His grace.

So please find your cathartic expression today! Read the Scripture, think of Joy (in the first volume of "Briefs") Jesus First, Others Second, Yourself Third. Give Give Give, and watch the waters flow out instead of backing up. Give Give Give, and experience the Joy of giving. Experience the Joy of helping. Experience the Joy of helping one to Heal as you seek to give in this life instead of taking.

So my conclusion is simple and direct. Get rid of your reservoir waste. Drain your psyche (or flesh, if you will). Refresh with new and living waters. "Be filled with the Holy Spirit" as Saul was when he became Paul, the Apostle (Acts 9: 17). It is your move! Make life pleasant for those with whom you are in contact!

God And The Jewish Peoples #47

There is a body of believers who have concluded that after the cross, God rescinded the Old Covenant, and replaced it with a new one, and therefore was finished with His Jewish people. A case can be made and argued for, that in the New Covenant, anyone can be saved, including Jews, and they are being saved slowly but surely. But some even go on to state God's covenant with Abraham had been broken at the cross negating the prophecies in the Old Testament.

My first reaction is that the Jewish people cannot dissolve (or break) that Old Covenant, since God put Abram to sleep when He exercised the covenant activities (Genesis 15). The strange thing is that the Jewish people of today operate as if they were an ungodly cult. For the most part they do not look to the Old Testament the Scriptures, but rather to the Talmud. They have often turned to the golden calf, Baal, Babylonian Kings, and rejected the Scriptures, and Christ. But the Scripture notes that they will return.

Christ takes the lead in my opinion, by focusing on Jewish reclamation. In Matthew 24: 14 & 15, He speaks of a time when the whole world will hear the Gospel. He speaks of the antichrist standing in the Holy Place (Sounds like the third Temple to me). In verse 21, He speaks of a worst-ever great tribulation (Revelation 6-19). If I return to Christ's point of reference, then I am in Daniel 9: 24-27. The angel Gabriel spells out the timeline to Daniel, for the activity of the Jewish people. This part of Daniel's prophecy, up to Christ, happened. The rest has not happened yet, including the Great Tribulation (The last seven years).

In the future, in Jerusalem, in the third Temple (Ezekiel 40-48) sacrifices will be made because, as it reads, when the antichrist moves in, sacrifices will be ended. People will also celebrate the Feast of Booths in remembrance (Zachariah 14: 16). Christ will rule from Jerusalem, and every country has to visit headquarters, or God will withhold rain from them! Sounds crazy to me, but read Zachariah 14: 17.

Lastly, go to Revelation 7 or 14. We see here that one hundred and forty four thousand Jewish evangelists will roam the earth evangelizing people. The "bondservants of God Almighty"! They "sing a new song". In the meantime, the Jews are a physical race. They have continued to be a stubborn and rebellious group before God, just as we were before salvation. There is something about us created human beings since Adam that needs be saved since Adam exercised his "free will" in the garden.

But, make no mistake my friend, God keeps His covenants. He will again bring forgiveness and salvation to this rebellious people. Bless them in your thinking, to avoid God's curse. As God promised Abraham before his conversion: "I will bless those who bless you, and the one who curses you, I will curse". "And in you all the families of the earth will be blessed". They are in a Jewish valley of anti-faith for a period due to a rejection of their Messiah, but get ready believers because our Jewish family and friends are:

Coming Back!

God And The Jewish Peoples #2 #48

I felt this topic was worth two visits, as the Jewish people will assuredly have the lead pony position in God's created humanity. I say this as these people keep showing up as predicted in the Scripture throughout known human history. Fantasies about life existing over millions of years are to me, just that. I always use the Bible as a point of reference for literal history as opposed to human speculation. History looks in the past. Science can only evaluate the present, and prophecy looks to the future.

Some make great hay over covenants. Paul does speak of the old and New Covenants in Romans 11. As a matter of fact, Romans 11 is the "go to" chapter that explains it totally. I do not think the average believer and accepter of the New Covenant, realizes that God entered into over three hundred covenants in the Bible. Check your concordance, or just "Google it". So it becomes obvious that covenants parallel sometimes instead of replacing. A major note revealed in Romans 11, is that God has a number in mind for gentile salvation. At that point He turns back to His chosen race.

I already noted passages speaking to God's actions and the Jews. Revelation 14 notes one hundred and forty four thousand evangelical Jewish (born-again) men are unleashed on society. They are listed as twelve thousand from each of the twelve tribes. Some tribes are known, and some are not. They are, however, known to God, our Creator, as the twelve Jewish tribes that He has picked for the future. God speaks and prophesies of the New Covenant in Isaiah 59: 20, 21. After Christ of course, the New Covenant will be available to all. The Jewish leadership and most of the race rejected their Messiah in 33 A.D., and turned to riches and the Talmud for the most part.

I think Christ spoke it well in John 5: 46, 47 when He stated "For if you believed Moses, you would believe Me, for he wrote of Me", "But if you do not believe his writings, how will you believe My words". Or one might say, if you do not believe Moses was the writer of the Torah's words, you certainly will not believe anything that I have to say to/for you.

So we can now see that God is still working with "His" people. They re-up in Isaiah, Jeremiah, Ezekiel, Daniel, Zachariah, and Revelation, as well as others. The covenants parallel one another, but we are encouraged/evangelized to the "new". Repent, dear reader. Board the train to salvation, happiness, and eternity with Jesus, and all our Jewish converts.

All Aboard!

The Lord Laughs #49

This happens to be one of my favorite verses: Psalm 2 2-4: "He who sits in the heavens; Laughs. "The Kings of the earth (Congress?) set themselves...against the Lord" (verse 2)!" God laughs? I think that bodes well for the future. Have you studied the Revelation at the end of the New Testament? When God finally ends His patience and mercy toward unbelief and unbelievers, it gets ugly. I do not think He is laughing anymore.

Do you remember the days of Noah? Jesus Christ did! (Matthew 24: 32-44). How about Sodom and Gomorrah? How about Jerusalem taking off to Babylon? How about 70 A.D. and the Temple's destruction? Prosperity comes and goes. Jubilee come and goes (Leviticus 25: 8-22). Humans forget because that is our nature. We only remember when we are saved with God's touch and we study His Word. It has been often said: "those who neglect history are condemned to repeat it".

Is Not That The Truth?

How about the arrogance of this world's spiritual leader: Satan himself?

Isaiah 14: 13, 14:

I Will Ascend To Heaven,

I Will Set My Throne On High,

I Will Set On The Mount Of Assembly,

I Will Ascend Above The Heights Of The Clouds,

I Will Make Myself Like The Most High!

Whatever happened to the snake? Whatever happened to Pharaoh? Whatever happened to Jezebel or Nebuchadnezzar? What happened to Herod or Judas? Whatever happened to Stalin or Hitler? Leaders of

Kingdoms and countries come and go. They are here for a time and gone. All show power, and a few show mercy. Without our Creator, none show love! God laughs.

My wife is upset as I enjoy laughing. It is cathartic for me. It happens more since I had a stroke 5 years ago. It is a change in emotions, and a change in my throat, physically. I have got to say, however, I have a good role model; do not ya think?

So study God's Word, and then watch a little TV news. Have yourself a good laugh when you see what World leaders are up to. Then do what God does:

Have yourself a good laugh!

Gun Control, Or The Ten Commandments? #50

As I write this "Brief", my country is recoiling from a mass murder in the State of Texas. The immediate response from some of the Nation's leaders is to again raise the issue of controlling guns. These are the same people who speak of controlling drugs and alcohol. These are the same leaders who are caught in lies, allow abortion, and disallow prayer in public schools. All these items are addressed in the Ten Commandments in Exodus 20 of the Old Testament.

In my lifetime our society has been released to live any way they wish. Marriage is no longer a sacred relationship as over half of them end in divorce. In this age of the ridiculousness, male and female genders have become a mental choice regardless of the obvious physical differences, or chromosomes. Lying has become a National pastime.

So what is wrong with a standard to follow, for people to live in harmony with one another? According to the Bible, the God of creation gave a man, named Moses, this set of rules/laws to ensure we would live in harmony, and not confusion. If God is indeed our Creator (Genesis 1: 1), then what is wrong with recognizing that and focusing on that? Why not take some time off and rest? In today's seven-day society, we never stop. Are we better off? What if everyone stopped murdering? We would have peace in the large cities again and an extra sixty three million people in society who were not eliminated prior to birth.

What all of this boils down to is that what is played up as the correct direction of society is in conflict with the truth of the Scripture. You cannot be an atheist and stop murder. You cannot be an atheist and stop stealing. When you try, you will not see an end to lying, thievery, or adultery, because there is no standard for chivalry. What it comes to, is that if it does not go against me, then I can live with it. As I swim in my community pool, we discuss the abhorrence of mass killings, or homelessness, or countries in war with one another. As long as it does not reach my suburb!

So what is the best methodology in society for gun control? Just repost, teach, and live the Ten Commandments. Our founders gave us that freedom of exercise at the beginning of our country. Over the years it has been forgotten. The problem is that the Creator, noted earlier, is alive and active. He gives us the freedom to choose our guidance (Joshua 24: 15). You choose today! Let's repost the Ten Commandments and live them. All of the societal woes which we abhor will diminish to perspective.

We can at least start with believers, at least in our interactions and fellowship. Love one another, honor God in all we do, and Live:

The Big Ten

Hearing #51

So what have you been listening to lately? What have you been hearing? Especially at home! I join a group of men where I live to shoot pool. As we are all up in decades, some have the physical limitation in the flesh for hearing. Most have that same problem in their spirit! The most common answer to a question in the group is "huh?" Or "what?" We just cannot hear as well as in the past.

That demonstrates the physical issue. The spiritual issue is also one of hearing. Paul speaks to this problem in Romans 10: 17. "So Faith comes from hearing". Listening in the Spirit is a blessing for those of us whom God has touched. Again in Galatians 3: 2 Paul writes "Did you receive the Spirit by works of the Law or by Hearing With Faith"?

Some Christian religions emphasize the need for living a good life. They go too far by attaching this emphasis on works to one's salvation. I could give you multiple verses to demonstrate that the biggest challenge in life for a God-believer is to live it out in good works that please our Creator. Just read the ending in each of Paul's epistles or, if you will, the Book of James. But these "good works" than are the result of salvation, and not the process toward.

So hearing (listening), is a key ingredient to the process of salvation, growth, and serving in faith! James exhorts us to be "quick to hear, (and) slow to speak" (James 1: 19). As I look back in my conscious memory of life, I have forgotten it for the most part. Et Tous? But I can succinctly remember multiple times that I was quick to speak, and slow to listen. That is the difference in my existence between being an all-conference athlete, an attorney, and a beloved son, husband, and father.

So let me encourage my grandkids for who my "Briefs" were motivated. As you move forward in your chapters of existence, give an ear to James. You will not cease to believe the difference it makes in relationships. I am a fan of that great theologian "Judge Judy"☺. She is constantly repeating to all the foolish people who give up their rights to her arbitration, that God gave you one mouth and two ears; use them in that proportion!

So I guess it is a Biblical, Godly mandate. It Works! Start today and activate your listening. If you do, then you will be blessed. You will be blessed by God, as we have read, and also by your fellow man. Life will not get easier, necessarily, but the process will improve. People love to be listened to. God loves it more. One final tip in the hearing/listening process, your marriage will lastingly more successful if you prove you are listening by learning this standard operation. When being questioned by one's spouse, the best Spirit Filled reply is always:

Yes Dear ☺

Inside Out #52

Pastor Mike gave a great illustration Sunday on the need to clean ourselves up a bit/lot. He rode his car over a stretch one time and had an engine cooling issue. As the check engine function malfunctioned, he drove on until the car overheated and ground to a halt. This finely cleaned and detailed car was beautiful on the outside, while it was destroyed from the inside.

In the first 23 verses of Mark 7, Christ covered the topic well for us. The disciples had come to eat without washing their hands in a proper way. The Pharisees had noticed and appealed to Christ over the infraction. Christ then quoted Isaiah 29: 13, "These people come near to me with their mouth, and honor me with their lips, but their hearts are far from me". Have you had the car washed and waxed lately, but neglected to change the oil?

Christ then chided them for trading God's Laws for men's laws. In verses 8 and 9, "You have a fine way of setting aside the commands of God in order to observe your own traditions. He then continues by using the example of honoring one's parents and its misuse. They had replaced a God's mandate on caring for parents, and allowing that care and giving to be used for the Temple treasury. This suited their greed, and was another way to garner funds.

In verse 15 then, Christ reverses the process. It is not what is on the outside that corrupts, but that which is inanimate from the inside. We call it the "flesh", and its deeds are listed in Galatians 5: 19-21. It is scary/sad when we finally realize where the process begins. James repeats and reminds us "But each one is tempted when he is carried away, and enticed by his own lust" (James 1: 14). So sin comes from within, and not from our upbringing or environment.

When the disciples asked for clarification later, He replied in verse 18, "are you so stupid, you do not get it" (that was a paraphrase). In verses 20-23, He finalizes His point and makes it clear; it all comes from the inside. Christianity points out the need for salvation, based on this premise. We are not basically good, but rather basically bad. There is no way to get around it scripturally, as these verses point out.

It is okay to polish up and detail your locomotion. But you had better check the engine on a regular basis. Keep your vehicle serviced (go to church), Fix what is broken (read the Scripture for guidance and pray), and if necessary, get a new engine:

Get Saved!

It Is Never Too Late #53

Our pastor Kyle gave a magnificent message Sunday from Isaiah 53 in the Old Testament. He focused on verses 10-12. God wrote this book about seven hundred years before Christ lived and travelled Israel. If one understands this prophecy, then it pictures the promised Messiah to come. He is pictured as the sacrificial lamb dying for the sins of mankind, and crushed, not for what he did, but for what we did. That is the whole message of the New Testament, we can never do enough to be forgiven for our disobedience to our Creator, and another's blood must needs be shed.

In Hebrews 2: 2 we read: "how shall we escape, if we ignore, such a great salvation"? Also, in verse 9: "But we see Jesus…now crowned with glory and honor, because He suffered death, so He might taste death for everyone". Again we get into that concept that without the shedding of blood, there is no forgiveness. Now if you are an "evolutionary", non-biblical creation believer, I realize this may sound extreme or kooky. But a student of the Scripture has learned over the years who God is, how He works, and what we need to believe, to please Him.

One guy, who came to realize the important of Christ's life and death, did it at the ending of his own life. He was referred to as the thief on the cross. As I write this "Brief", we are experiencing "smash and grab" thieves in cities where they walk in a store, smash display cases, and leave with thousands of dollars' worth of stolen goods. We do nothing at this time. In Jesus day, they crucified them. It really cut back on the thieves running around.

This guilty thief had the true "come to Jesus" moment. In Luke 23: 39-43, the story is described as one criminal mocks Jesus and states if He is who He says, to take them down from their crosses. The other rebukes him and recognizes Jesus' innocence. Christ forgives him and promises the thief's salvation; today! Get it? Today is your salvation based on repenting for a life of disobedience and rule breaking. You might describe it as a complete reversal of attitude.

When you read the Isaiah passage then you see God's role in this whole program as it is the "Lord's will", and the "Lord Makes", and the "will of the Lord", and "He will see", and "I will give", and "He will divide", and "He bore the sin of many". You see dear reader, God is totally aware of the program in its entirety. He created it, managed it, and brought it to fruition seven hundred years later. Our Lord and Savior endured it for us. Hebrews 12: 2 "who for the Joy set before Him, endured the cross". Get it? Get it!

So my friend, it is never too late. Christ's sacrifice for you, was predicted, processed, and finalized. But Christ then rose from the dead three days later, ministered to people for a couple months, and left like a rocket ship: Acts 1. What we are talking about here is a change in attitude. The thief did it on His final day! I would not wait, however, because you cannot predict that day and you do not want to be a day late.

That is a pretty heavy trip that I just shared. If you drive a car in Arizona, you will pass a gas station, treat shop regularly. They have descriptively named it "Quick Trip" as it takes a quick decision for the quick trip. When you leave this planet, it will be a "quick trip". Do not wait until that day.

Change your attitude now! Ask for forgiveness! Make your "quick trip" Today! ☺

Jesus Birth Prophesized #54

I am writing this "Brief" during the Christmas week. In two days we will head off to California to celebrate this earth shattering event by the ocean. We will drive over in a car. Christ had no such luxury. As a matter of fact, He was born in the lamest place God could find, surrounded by smelly animals. What must Mary have thought after all the events leading up to this time?

Getting pregnant just by being the one picked, she was betrothed and I am sure this virgin teenager had wondered about the process of love and attachment she would soon know. But she also knew she was with child, and she did not have any reason to be, had Gabriel not have explained it to her. Believable, or unbelievable? How about the trek from Nazareth to Bethlehem? In a limo? Sorry, it was on the back end of a donkey. Then there was no room in the Inn so they set up base in the barn and birthed the promised Messiah. Wow, that is bazaar!

So let's go back seven hundred years and see what God predicted. Micah 5: 2-5 covers the program for Bible believers. I do not think evolutionists would say life was improving for the Joseph during this period. Anyway, verse 2 starts with: "But you Bethlehem". Then it continues: "out of you will come for me one who will be ruler over Israel". Then it says, "And the rest of His brothers return". Lastly in verse 4 it states, "And they will live securely, for then His greatness will reach to the ends of the earth". It all begins in Bethlehem, and it did. Easy to say now as we know historically that it took place.

So the prophecy covers the whole gamut. Some of it is yet to come, but the beginning was exact: "O little town of Bethlehem". Also in Isaiah 7: 14+ we read "Immanuel" (God with us), will be born of a virgin. The Jewish people have now returned to Israel, and getting ready for the balance of the prophecy. At some point in time (and I think soon), the Lord will return and set up His rule, after His judgment.

So this has not been some haphazard set of events. Rather it is as well-planned and orchestrated as the rotation of the earth, the appropriately distanced sun, moon, and stars. Did you think all this happened by accident? Darwin did! And so do all Darwin's Godless followers today. But I got lucky. I chose to follow the Bible, cover to cover.

God created it. God manages it. God controls it. And I was chosen to be on the team!

Wanna Join? ☺

Life's Essentials: Breathing, Drinking, And Resting #55

Have you often thought of what you take for granted? If you did, then you would unquestionably believe in the need for your Creator. We breath, we drink, and we sleep without considerable thought. We accept our parentage, ancestry, and relationships as rather automatic, and traditional. I thought of this after a beautiful night of sleep that I appreciated and did not take for granted. I awoke, not needing to get to the office, start the commute, or catch a plane for the other coast.

How often do you stop to consider the air that you breathe? Do you consciously separate the oxygen out that is necessary for your blood system? Do you consider in moments of breathing, the filtering process in your lungs to remove particulates? Again, we have life functions that God has created for us to operate in an automatic process for our wellbeing.

How often do you stop to consider the need for fresh processed water in your life? I moved to the Arizona desert a decade ago, which is dependent on water, originating in the State of Colorado. As I write this "Brief", the collecting basin in Lake Powel, has become dangerously low in supply. Is it possible that we are in a potential drought era, where we can no longer depend on the automatic supply I have enjoyed in my lifetime?

"In the beginning God created the heavens and the earth" (Genesis 1: 1). "Let there be an expanse in the midst of the waters, and let it separate the waters from the waters" (Genesis 1: 6). "Let the waters below the heavens be gathered into one place, and let the dry land appear; and it was so". So the truth of Creation is covered in the very first chapter of the Bible as God created air, water, and land! Do you just take that for granted? Eighty percent of the world's population does today!

So how about the concept, need for, reality of, our rest? God considered it so important, that it was included in the Ten Commandments: "the seventh day is a Sabbath (Rest) of the Lord your God…and rested on the seventh day" (Exodus 20: 8-11). Hebrews 4: 1-11 covers the subject quite well. The inference/revelation is that future point of eternal "rest" just as Joshua had noted the "rest" being entered into as the Israelites entered the Promised Land in Joshua 22.

So do not be anxious, dear reader, but do appreciate, our sheepish (stupid?) minds assume the realities of clean air, fresh water, and continual rest. These God provisions are seemingly automatic and dependent only on human creation and interaction. A good attitude about our provisions coming from our Creator would be a major paradigm shift from the modern assumptions of climate change espoused by political, Godless leadership today.

So my dear created friend, please stop for periodic moments as you thank God for life and your personal existence. Thank God for the air we breathe, the water we drink, and the seven hours of sleep you enjoy.

Breath, drink, and sleep! They are a gift from your creator!

Job Living Faith #56

No greater man has lived through the trials of life then the man named Job. An entire book is dedicated to his life in the Old Testament just before the book of Psalms. It is noted to be the first transcribed text of the Old Testament, but all dating is speculative. That is not a point of importance to me, but rather the faith of this great man as God allowed his tortured-life, and his resurrected blessings.

Does it Make You Think Of Anyone?

Chapter 1 is not only interesting, it is amazing. My learning and acceptance of the Scripture is the process of processing from the known to the unknown. I cannot say that I always accepted the earth's Creation happening in six days (Genesis 1), but today, I have no doubt. I cannot say that I always believed in Christ's ascension right in front of the disciples (Acts 1), but today I have no doubt. I cannot say that I always believed that Christ's birth in Bethlehem was predicted seven hundred years prior to the date, but today it is a known fact. Ever wonder why a pregnant woman in her eighth month would ride a donkey sixty to eighty miles so her husband could pay his taxes? It is because Micah prophesied it. I will bet Joseph got an earful on that trip.

In one day, Job lost everything he owned from family, to livestock, to buildings, and in chapter 2, his good health as well. God allowed all this to make a point to Satan and God's creation. This man of faith was stripped of everything good this life can offer, and Satan was "allowed" to strip Job of everything but his personal existence. Through this, God would prove Job's abiding faith. Does this sound as though God does not get involved in the intimate details of one's life?

I now realize the story's purpose: God is intimately involved in our lives. In 1: 21 Job states: "the Lord gave, and the Lord has taken away" He had no doubt in the beginning and midst of his tortured experience. Have you gone through that? I lost my firstborn. I lost a business. I had a full-blown stroke. These were minor compared to Job, but not when they occurred to me. Job later states in 5: 17: "So do not despise the discipline of the Almighty". Do you get it?

This process we live through (life), gives us three score and ten years, on average, to get the picture clarified concerning our creation, and our Creator. He gave us a book to study that Job did not have. Have you ever read it? God calls it His Word (the Bible). In Acts 2: 41 we read: "those who had received His Word were baptized". Baptism is a part of God's marketing program and an essential, not for salvation but obedience! God likes obedience! (1 Samuel 15: 22).

Let people know what is happened in your life. You do not need to lose everything like Job did. God proved His point already. But let your life mature in faith and knowledge. Do not just grow older. Grow Up!

The last chapters of this book are amazing statement of Faith, in "both" directions. Have a read! Maybe then you will also say, based on your life experience:

JOB 42: 5 "But Now My Eye Sees Thee" ☺

Love Or Fear #57

The Apostle John matured to be one of or, the, greatest Apostle of Love. John 3 is the most conclusive Book in the New Testament concerning what it takes to gain God's Kingdom and proceed to Heaven and everlasting Glory: "You must be born again"! His three other Epistles of first, second, and third John, ice the cake. And what a beautiful cake it is. In first John 4: 18 we read: "There is no fear in love, but perfect love casts out fear".

It seems then the opposite of love becomes fear. What are you afraid of? Getting hit? Getting fired? Getting dumped? Dying? All of those things and many more have come up in the recent and current pandemic. I personally believe God brought this pandemic on as he did former plagues, droughts, and depressions. It is a great way to separate the sheep from the goats, believers from non-believers, and assuredly get more humans saved.

So the devil certainly uses fear as a modus operandi. Where does he operate? "From going to and fro on the earth" (Job 1-7, Job 2: 2). Do you question Satan's given power? Read the account of Jesus' temptation in Matthew 4: 1-11. The devil "took" Jesus twice to various locations. Satan entered the body/person of Judas (John 13: 27). Yes, Satan has a power to control things, enter into people, and come and go at will. But we have the power to "submit yourselves therefore to God. Resist the devil and he will flee from you" (James 4: 7). Do not try to turn those around.

Have you ever watched a drama movie or a horror one? I hate horror movies and never turn to them. They work on fear, and I know the author. When I am not in submission to my Creator, the fear can be overwhelming. That was the power of the 2020 pandemic. It was a fear of death. A lot of people did die as the virus attacked old people, sick people, and overweight people. By the time money and politics got involved and overwhelmed the program, it was sad.

So which direction will you choose? The old fable of us having a good wolf and a bad wolf comes to thought. The one you feed will overwhelm you, and control you. If you live in submission and study God's Word, then you will "know the truth, and the Truth will set you free" (John 8: 32). If you do not, then, well, you can expect a world fraught with fear!

Enjoy Your Love Trip ☺

Make God Happy #58

I was reading a daily, this AM, authored by the notable Christian author Oswald Chambers. The booklet is entitled "My Utmost for His Highest". Dailies are great and written by pastors such as Max Lucado, David Jeremiah, John MacArthur, and different women authors depending on gender interest or Jesus-based theology.

 In this one, Oswald noted God's reminder to the prophet Jeremiah in 2: 2, "I remember the kindness of your youth". After life toughens you up, you lose some of that soft touch. Is not that why marriages fail, and friendships disappear? Chambers went on to say: "Does everything in my life fill His heart with gladness, or do I constantly complain"? "A person, who has forgotten what God treasures, will not be filled with Joy". "How much kindness have I shown Him in the past week"?

I checked my concordance and discovered to my surprise that it has a few "happies" listed. During a quick perusal of my three translations, I discovered that all three used the translation "blessed". I like "Happy". It is sort of like when people say Happy New Year on January first. I like to reply Joyful New Year! But take your pick: happy or blessed; they are both listed there.

I have seen a definite progression in friends and acquaintances. You can definitely experience it in family relations. One cools on/toward God, then it is the parents/family (Exodus 20: 12, the fifth), then it is the spouse, then it is the fellow workers, and so forth. The whole issue "to me" is making God happy! If you could care less, then everything else starts to fall apart as you move up to your throne. One problem in a prosperous society is that God can progressively be replaced by money (mammon), and it is a major paradigm shift as they say. Divorce is not so bad now, as you have material wealth to divide.

Let's cut to the chase! Christ appealed to His Father just before Judas betrayed Him (Luke 23: 42) "…not my will, but thine be done". So that is the ultimate submission. Jesus (God the Son) made His Father happy. He made the disciples unhappy in the immediate. But He made all of us who trust in Him, extremely happy. So start at the top and work backwards. Put it down as a list on paper, if necessary!

If I am not making God happy, then how can I make anyone on my list happy? My spouse? My family? My co-workers? My neighbors? We may be touching on the arena of attitude folks. If I cannot get it right with my Creator, then how can I come close with my created? Some people can take irritations, and create pearls. Oysters do! Some people just get eaten in the process.

Believe God. Trust in Him. Seek to please Him and make Him happy. Everyone else will fall in line.

If people irritate you, make pearls! God Does!

Open Your Eyes #59

I was "led" to read Deuteronomy chapters 8-12 this morning. Now that is just crazy. I had finished my AM pool exercise class surrounded by tall palms and fellow resort-living friends, discussing past and upcoming vacations and cruises. I had also just checked my cell phone, and read about twenty Christians in Nigeria who were forced to their knees, and shot to death. For Their Faith In Christ??? What a contrast!

These words in the Bible's Old Testament were spoken to the wandering Israelites before they entered the Promised Land. We know that it is before because we know that Moses did not get to enter across the Jordan River. Moses' great monologue/preachment covered recent history (the past forty years), and all the key events in the Hebrew Exodus from Egypt. It also emphasized God's power and the need for the Israelites to heed that power and depend on God, and Him alone. Please read these chapters to fully understand.

God used those forty years to educate and purge the generation that closed its eyes. Do not be upset with parents, children, or grandchildren. Open "Your" Eyes! Moses pointed out the historic happenings, such as the parting and closing of the Red Sea, the creation and destruction of the golden calf, and the earth opening to swallow up thousands of those who disbelieved. God does not do this every year! He did it with the Israelites so that generations to come might be warned of His power in your personal activities. Ask Noah, or David, or Samson, or Gideon, or Elijah, or Daniel, or Paul, or your mirror and memory. Get my drift?

Have you taken the Exodus trip? Have you repented? Have you traveled through life rejecting God's Love, tracking your own path and destiny? I am amazed at our chutzpah! Do not we know that each and every one of us passes on? You know, dies? Getting right with our Creator then, is nothing new. But it is a mandate. We all die

(Hebrews 9: 27), and we all resurrect in one direction or the other (Daniel 12: 2)

So these Deuteronomy chapters are a must-read. Moses was unbelievable. He twice ascended to Mount Sinai, and did not eat for forty days and nights, while he was over eighty years old. That is quite a diet at any age! I will add, however, that in the presence of God, nourishment takes on a new twist. I cannot wait. If you study this quick history, dear reader, then you will get the full picture. Be the person who opens your mind and spirit. Do what your Creator wants you to do. That is what these "Briefs" are all about. Take that first step however, and assuredly:

Open Your Eyes! ☺

Our Traveling Salesman #60

Now, that is the last description one would ever use to describe Jesus. But I get it! If you do not believe, then it check out Mark 1: 32-39. "That is why I have come". Those are Jesus' words to His disciples. He had just spent a hard day at work, healing people and driving out demons. You know, I get the healing part because people still need healing. But I am really concerned about that demon possession part. I know a few people……. Oh1 never mind.

So Pastor Tad focused on this passage, and Jesus "the travelling salesman" said "let's go somewhere else -to the nearby villages- so I can preach there also". I mean that people were lining up already for healing and relief, when His statement was, "let's get outta here. I have a program to sell" (That was a paraphrase). They left and He went elsewhere in Galilee, preaching in Synagogues as well as healing. I do know He was wired in to the father since He got up real early, and went to the hills to pray.

You do realize that they did not have hospitals back then? If you got real sick, then you were on your way out. If you contracted Leprosy, then they sent you to colonies out of town and you could not come back. Jesus just touched them, and all was well. Just read the chapter a little further. Today we take healing for granted. We do not just need one guy to be there, we have hundreds of thousands of doctors and nurses trained with amazing equipment to work with. Do you take that for granted? Do you not see that as a gift from God?

So Jesus understood the basics of good management; first things first! He also understood good delegation. But I believe that He was trying to communicate His timeline. He had three years of ministry to do, and it was time to move on. He was one man at the time, and He needed more people to experience His presence ASAP.

Tad determined than, that preaching superseded healing. Well it is a Baptist church after all. I believe that they think that Jesus turned the water into grape juice. ☺ Anyway, actions speak louder than words,

119

and he may be correct. I tend to think Christ was saying that they have seen me in this town, they have witnessed my Holy touch, and enough is enough. Let's move on!

Christ healed a leper, He healed a paralytic, and He chose the rest of the disciples. He was a busy man, and He had the Gospel to preach. I spent a few years on the road, and I get it. If you do not show up, then no one learns about your product. I worked the "come and see it" program forty years ago, before we were computer dependent, when TV screens were barely in color, and we did not have cell phones. Holy Smoke am I that old. ☹

So Christ moved on. He preached and healed in continuing locations (read the Gospels) and He closed the deals. I taught my sales teams to always give the customer a chance to say Yes. Has that changed? Was not it true in Christ's time?

 Travel my reader! Preach the Gospel! And give the people a chance to say: Yes!

Robed In Love #61

Robes can be a beautiful covering. They price to all levels when purchased. It depends on everything from the quality of the robe, to the woven material, to the weave, and to the softness. They always are used to cover one level of nakedness or another, but in the Scriptures we see one is covered by God's Love, and the covering analogy really applies.

The first couple, needed forgiveness, right off the bat. All they did was the one thing God told them not to do (Genesis 3: 21) They tried to fix it themselves (sound familiar?), but God had other plans. They tried using vegetation (plant growth), but God was not interested. Right in the beginning, God demanded a blood (life substitute) sacrifice to atone for their disobedience. Off came the fig leaves, on came the animal skins!

Another story in Luke 15, is the parable of the Prodigal son. After totally blowing everything material, the son who wasted his inheritance, came home. His father was overjoyed that his son had repented and returned, so he called for a giant celebration and killed the "fatted calf". As a part of the festivity he called the slaves to: "quickly bring out the "best" robe and put it on him" (Luke 15: 22). One might say that the robe covered his degenerate body and sin sufferings.

In Revelation 7: 14, we see an enormous crowd worshipping God at His throne, and when John asked who they were, an angel replied that "these are the ones who come out of the Great Tribulation, and they have washed their "robes" and made them white in the blood of the Lamb". Again we see the covering of the "robe"; a long loose outer garment.

Have you been covered? Has God covered you? In none of the three examples above did the initiative seem to originate in the recipient. Did you accept and receive your gift? It is humbling when understood. In the Revelation, they seemed to have washed their robes. Adam and

Eve did not! The prodigal knew that he had blown it, and did not deserve it. In any case appreciate and enjoy it.

But By All Means My Friend, Receive A Robe!

Seeding #62

I think we get too enamored in the process of sharing the Gospel, with the part which we play. Some folks go all the way with human intervention to the point where we have to personally carry the burden to get people the message, close the sale (I had a career in sales), and lay hands on people for their salvation. I think the Bible paints a different picture. This morning Pastor Chuck touched on the program of seeding in Mark 4.

Our job is to bring our "light" from under the bed or basket, and not hide the "Good News". Across Mill Street from the church in Temple, are fifty thousand students being fed daily, a gospel of self-reliance, anti-God, anti-Baby, and anti-Love (Agape'). It is amazing how much money students and parents will pay, just to pack their brains with anti-Biblical positions. The Bible says God created everything (Genesis 1: 1), He knit us in the womb (Jeremiah 1: 5), and Jesus really did exist! (Matthew, Mark, Luke, John) At present you will not hear that at ASU, but they formerly taught theology at Harvard, Yale, and Princeton!

So what is our role then but to scatter seed? In Mark 4: 26-29 we read the process! Throw the seed out, some will germinate and grow, but I think Jesus was saying that is God's job. We come back in when it is time for the harvest. Get It? "Put the sickle to it because the harvest has come".

Earlier I heard from Costi teaching 1 Peter 4: 7-11. Check your attitude, timing, initiative, or persistence at the door for "the end…is near! Be clear-minded and controlled…so that you can pray… Love each other deeply…offer hospitality…without grumbling…each one should use whatever gift he has received to serve others…speak the very Words of God…do it with the strength God supplies…so that God may be praised".

Jesus closed in Mark 4: 30-32 with the parable of the mustard seed. It is the smallest of all seeds to be planted, and yet grows to be a tree five to six times the height of a man. Do you sometimes feel insignificant in the program of planting trees? If you later returned and found an orchard of mustard trees, would you have felt over-exercised and under-productive? I think not! If you continue to plant insignificantly sized seeds, then you are doing your assigned task. If you get discouraged and quit seeding, then or quit planting, there will be nothing to harvest.

Stay strong, stay focused, enjoy your role, and pray God to exercise His! And then:

Get Ready To Harvest! ☺

Spell Checking My Life #63

We spent the evening with my wife's brother and wife at a local resort that was set up for Christmas. With all the lights, rides, and music, it was a festive atmosphere and a great introduction to the Christmas season. I might add however, not any reference to the advent season, as I recall. As we lounged in outdoor furniture, viewing the array of lights and carousels, my brother-in-law suggested a new "Brief" idea, that he liked going into the New Year. Please enjoy the following.

As I create these "1 Page Briefs" on my computer, I am aided by multiple tools for perfection and correction. I am so old that we did not have computers when in college. I could not change paragraphs, and for sure, could not spellcheck. He suggested that I comment on the Bible as the spellcheck for our lives. This was a point well made, and a thought for the next year. Have you considered that as a technique for living in the present? Let me suggest where one might go to find daily, weekly, and annual guidance.

Let me first suggest, as I did years ago to my grandkids, that you consider Genesis 1: 1. Who is God? Our Creator! Start there and build, or you will have no foundation. Next, consider the Gospels. We read here about Jesus Christ, God in the flesh, and all He has to say about planning one's life, living it, and what to expect in your future. He notes that we have significant problems with correctness, and lays out the plans for correction, and then expounds on and lives out His role in the corrective process.

Jesus Is Our Spellcheck, If You Will. He Is Not, If You Will Not!

I believe the place to go for the dailies, however, are to the Old Testament books referred to as poetry; Psalms and Proverbs. Psalms are seen in light of man/women relating to their Creator/God, and Proverbs as people relating to other people. Just pick some out randomly, and you will see what I mean. For example try Psalm 23, "And picture God/Christ as your Shepherd". Proverbs 13 will give you some good plan and action ideas for getting through life in society.

Lastly (if not firstly☺) consider the Ten Commandments. Having a bad day, week, month, or year? I have had my share. Praying for correction? Family issues? Job issues? Is it possible you have sworn your Creator's name? Is it possible you told a little white lie, stolen something (like cheating on taxes)? Is it possible you have coveted something a friend or neighbor has like a better car, bigger house, or a stock that went through the roof? Why not go to these ten simple rules and just make the necessary corrections.

So I think you get the point! Make your corrections, and just move on. Our culture can drive you nuts with temptation, attacks, and a constant drip, drip, dripping of desire and temptation. Everything you need is listed above to help correct life's misspellings. The Psalms, Proverbs routine is amazing. The Gospels routine is enlightening and educational. The goal is that as one ages and matures, the spelling will improve.

Learn the process, dear reader. Get corrected as your Creator would love. When you are finished with this brief life, you might just love and appreciate the finished product.

I Know Your Creator Will ☺

Sufferings #64

I have friends who have suffered and are suffering! The pain of degenerative cancer without insurance! Parkinson's disease! Sequestered to a wheelchair after years of good health and workouts! A mosquito's sting and death two weeks later occurred for a friend! My own stroke, five years ago, with my wife pushing my wheelchair, and my inoperative left arm.

Suffered lately? Check out what the Apostle Paul went through in 2 Corinthians 11: 16+: "imprisoned…five times forty lashes…three times, beaten with rods…once stoned…three times shipwrecked…a night and day in the open sea…" Besides everything else, I face the pressure of my daily concern for all the churches.

When you read about Paul's experience, you have to question his persistence and tenacity. But he had seen Christ on the Damascus road (Acts 9), and was taken up to the third heaven (2 Corinthian 12: 2) shortly thereafter. He was motivated by his amazing experiences in reality.

Focus on Jesus! Then read 2 Corinthians 4: 16-18: "Therefore we do not lose heart. Though outwardly we are wasting away, yet inwardly we are being renewed day by day. For our light and momentary troubles are achieving for us an eternal glory, that far outweighs them all. So we fix our eyes not on what is seen, but on what is unseen. For what is seen is temporary, but what is unseen is eternal".

Have you read the last two chapters of the Bible a few times? (Revelation 21, 22) I am sorry my friend, I cannot wait to get there. Paul said: "For to me, to live is Christ, and to die is Gain" (Philippians 1: 21). The whole idea then is to live through your suffering, grow from it, build you faith in God's mercy and graciousness, and gain from it. Can a butterfly exist without passage through the cocoon?

Look, I do not make the rules, God does! How about Paul, how about Peter, how about the Johns, and of course, how about Jesus??? It is no fun, of course, but it is a process. We have, on the other hand, been saved and blessed and can appreciate the end goal for us. The cocoon develops, but the butterfly emerges! It is an ugly process, but a beautiful result. Few women will tell you that they love the process, but all will tell you that they love the result of bearing a child.

When You Suffer Dear Reader, You Will Be Rewarded!

Sugar Or Jesus? #65

Now that seems to be an interesting choice to ponder. But is it? I live in, have lived in, and probably will live in, until my ending, the suburbs of America. I have heard stats that ninety nine percent of the world makes less income than I do in my retirement. At the same time, we Americans, on average, eat +/- 150s of refined sugar each year (we raise the average, you know). Now I know the sin of too much alcohol, or drugs, or tobacco. But sugar?

I am currently reading a paperback on that subject: "The 40 day Sugar Fast", by Wendy Speake. She has expertly woven in The Scripture with thoughts about cutting back, if not cutting out sugar. Have you ever stopped to think about the time and money our prosperous society spends on eating? The best restaurants, the best snacks, the best desserts! Over half of USA meals are eaten out in this generation. Most prepared foods that we consume contain sugar. All of the largest drinking companies have learned how to "can up" sugar and soda to our delight and diabetic downfall. We are addicted!

The Bible is loaded with verses on the topic of Fasting. In all the examples of seeking God's Grace, people fasted and prayed. Have you done that lately? How many skinny pastors do you see leading their flocks around? I refer to food today as "mouth entertainment". I am discouraged by how programmed I have made myself to taste buds as opposed to "body buds". What my mouth hors d'oeuvres, my body deplores.

Do you trust in Jesus? That is the real challenge. It was for Jehoshaphat in 2 Chronicles 20. Judah was being attacked by the same armies that God told Moses to avoid back in the Exodus. Their sons were born and had grown, and now returned to wipe out the Israelites. Jehoshaphat led the people to fast, and prayed to God for deliverance. The results were astonishing as the enemy turned on themselves and were destroyed. "The battle is not yours, but God's" (verse 15).

So it is a Spiritual battle than! Fill your body, or fill your Spirit. I do not recall Jesus saying, "Stuff your gut, and pray". When Jesus began His ministry, He fasted for forty days (Matthew 4: 2). When Moses picked up the Ten Commandments, he fasted for forty days. I really wish that I was that Spiritual. I wish my Pastors were. I wish my President was, and my Legislators were, and the Supreme Judges of the land were! Back to reality! For the next forty days, I can, at least fast from sugar. Or can I? If I replace sugar with Jesus, then I will.

What I like about this challenge is that if successful, then my new shirts will fit. Secondly, my blood tests will please my Doctor. Thirdly, I like to think that I will be more Jesus-focused in these turbulent times so that maybe the loss of foodstuff will not concern me as much. ☺ Sadly or thankfully, it is a choice that I can make. I can eat more sugar and die, or I can eat less sugar and live (longer)! As Paul so aptly stated in Philippians 1: 21:

"For To Me To Live Is Christ, And To Die Is Gain"!

Think I will go live a little…

The Good Shepherd #66

It was a great weekend of ministry for me. I attend different churches like some people go to movies, or baseball games. Different strokes for different folks (As I say to those of you learning a golf swing☺). I will begin in reverse order as Pastor Chuck explained the picture of sheep and shepherds. Sheep are apparently pretty stupid. The key is for the shepherd is to lead them to green pastures. When finished in their mowing of the field, they will stay there and starve even if new grass is a short distance away. Hence, the need for good shepherding to lead them to the next pasture.

When Jesus fed the five thousand, He led them to sit on grassy areas (John 6: 10). Coincidence? Everything in The Scripture has a purpose! Our great provider, shepherd, took everything into account, from the need to eat, to the seating arrangements. "I am the good shepherd" (John 10: 11).

Earlier, I heard Pastor Costi as he asked for prayer for his new flock. He went so far as to solicit his wife's prayers for his message that Sunday, as Christ would have asked for the disciple's prayers. Me? I just show up and enjoy the good preaching (green grass). Costi has a new ministry and prays for God's blessing, and his shepherding. He focused on Acts 20, and Paul's departing remarks to the Elders from the churches he had established. In Acts 20: 17-38, Paul was leaving town with a bucket full of tears and good wishes. He warned his herd to look out for the wolves who would attempt to fill his space. Costi felt that in his message as he approached his series on the Book of Ephesians (that great Epistle of theology and fellowship).

Pastor Jon rather sealed the deal for me on Saturday evening, the night before. He focused on John 3: 17-21. This passage focuses on God's salvation for believers. Jon's exhortation was to 1) Be humbled by God's rescuing us (believers), 2) Own it and be rescued from ourselves, and 3) recognize that your life validates your faith. John hits on light and darkness in this passage. Without Christ, we have no light! Praise God continually for salvation and the light it creates in our lives. It is the greatest miracle, indeed.

Now you can appreciate the trilogy of faith: Believe in your Creator; seek the/a good Shepherd, and "Own It". Psalm 23 encapsulates the entirety of our Faith! For me, "The Lord is my shepherd". I love hearing about it, feeding off of it, sharing with others over it, and facing life and it is ending with it. Find the "Good Shepherd" today, if you have not yet. Find a good shepherd in local fellowship if you have not yet. I will guarantee you that:

The Grass Is Greener, On Both Sides Of The Fence!

The Hyssop Branch #67

This plant caught my attention as it was the one used when Christ was given vinegar to drink on the last stages on the cross. I have not thought much about this over the years, and why should I have? Is not that the way with The Scripture? After agreement on the gospel faith we Christians adhere to, our personalities take us in all sorts of directions. Hence, Denominations? Not cults, or unchristian belief systems, but Christ-followers, born-again, and looking toward the everlasting. We form opinions on baptism, end times, and the exercise of charisma today.

At any rate, this plant is also mentioned during the Exodus plagues (Exodus 12: 22). It was the plant that was dipped in blood to spread on the mantles to dissuade the angel of death from entering the Jewish households. Get It? This absorbent plant spread the protective blood of the lambs, and years later was used to satisfy the thirst of the ultimate Lamb of God.

Why Hyssop? It is a plant that grows in the Middle East, and is apparently absorbent. But to use the same one that was used for the Passover and then for our Savior as He exited the World as "our" Passover through Faith? What a coincidence? ☺ Hyssop is associated with cleansing. There are multiple references to this as in Psalm 51: 7: "Purify me with Hyssop and I shall be clean". This verse was in the context of Spiritual cleansing.

Solomon referred to hyssop at the outset of his kingship. At that time he had not yet yielded to his flesh, and had the abundance of wives and concubines. In this context he displayed amazing wisdom and knowledge. I believe the Hyssop notice was for the same reason of the Passover references around Moses and Jesus. I stopped to read a few chapters around I Kings 1-4, and this boy was rich. The Kingdom stretched from the Euphrates River to Egypt; or what God had prophesied to Abraham.

So we can see that it was no "coincidence" in John 19: 28 that Christ said "I am thirsty". He wanted to bring the hyssop branch into the picture for the Spiritual cleansing provided by His sacrifice. I am tempted to order the essential oil of this plant as a symbol of my salvation as I pray (so I did). It would at least be a reminder of this beautiful bush and its Biblical reference. It would remind me in or for the future that indeed:

I Am Cleansed!

The Jesus Hospital #68

It did not take Jesus long after His baptism, to get started with His ministry. The first thing He did was to throw a party. Well, not exactly. But He did join one, with His mother's approval where she is quoted as saying "Whatever He says to you, do it" (John 2: 5). He then had the servants take six stone jars and fill them with water. These jars each held twenty to thirty gallons apiece, and He miraculously changed the water into wine. I do not care how many people attended, but that is a lot of wine folks. How about umpteen cases of Gallo, but much finer and a lot more expensive?

Now I realize, this is one miracle that my Baptist friends wish He had skipped. As a matter of fact, His critics accused Him of being a wine-bibber (drunk) when He partied (Matthew 11: 19). Wine was not all that bad back then as the alcohol also had good medicinal characteristics (1 Timothy 5: 23). We were however instructed to take it easy when drinking wine (Ephesians 5: 18), so in college, I stuck to beer!

The big event for Capernaum was when Jesus came to town and opened the first hospital. He was the great physician, you know! Mark 2: 17 rather sums it up. He stated "It is not those who are healthy who need a physician, but those who are sick; I did not come to call the righteous, but sinners". He first came to Peter and Andrew's house, healed their mother of a fever, and she went to the kitchen and cooked dinner.

Well the word got out, and people started coming over (Mark 1: 33). "The whole city had gathered at the door". Bingo, Capernaum had a hospital. Jesus began healing people and casting out demons, right and left. By morning He was exhausted, and they moved on; He and the initial disciples. Everywhere Christ went, He healed people. That power is gone as an activity although some try to play with the concept. Healing is not gone, and God outlined the process through James: "Is any among you sick, let him call for the elders of the church, and let them pray over him, anointing him with oil in the name of the Lord, and the prayer offered in faith will restore the one who is sick…" (James 5: 14, 15).

When Jesus predicted His leaving, He promised God the Holy Spirit. So much more would be done by so many more as the Holy Spirit came on, and in, His followers and believers. When you go to the hospital do you thank God and the physicians? Hospitals were set up by Christians many decades ago. Healing is performed by hundreds of thousands of trained staff and scientific equipment. Without God the Creator, none of this science would exist, including the "earth" on which we exist.

I close with a crazy story. As God led the Jewish people to freedom, some complained and moaned about the dessert conditions. I get it because I live in Arizona! It said in Numbers 21 that the Lord sent venomous snakes to bite the "bitch-ers". As the rest screamed for help, God had Moses put a bronze snake on a pole, and all who looked up at that snake were saved. The next time you go to a hospital, look for that snake. It is there, even today. The Godless give credit to Greek mythology, but believers recount the real story from Numbers!

Look Up And Be Healed!

The Great Physician Is Still At Work (in multiple locations)☺

The Last Trinity #69

It occurred to me as pastor Tad outlined the three most important elements in a believer's life, that we had just covered the third of the "threes": the Trinity of the Godhead, the Trinity of the Church, and now the Trinity for the believer. First: the Father, Son, and Holy Spirit, second: Theology, Fellowship, and Ministry, and now third: Prayer, the Word, and Fellowship.

We are never given the Trinity in The Scripture as a singular definition anywhere. But the educated, mature believer can easily ascertain its reality. God the Father is easy: "Our Father, who art in Heaven, hollowed be thy name" (Matthew 6). God the Son follows: "but He was even calling God His own Father, making Himself equal with God" (John 5: 18), and lastly God the Holy Spirit: "you have lied to the Holy Spirit. You have not lied to men, but to God" (Acts 5).

With the "Ecclesia" than, we see those "called out" (a church group), to be taught and matured in the faith. He gave us Pastors and teachers to give us the Word (Ephesians 5). He leads us to fellowship! (Hebrews 10: 25) And lastly we are lead to ministry: "Religion that God our Father accepts as pure and faultless is this; to look after orphans and widows in their distress" (James 1: 27). So our church "Trinity" then, is to lead with Theology, relate in a fellowship, and lastly give to others less fortunate as our ministry.

Paul encourages us to "hold fast to the Word I preached to you" (1 Corinthians 1: 2). Hebrews 10: 25 motivates us: "not neglecting to meet together, as is the habit of some, but encouraging one another...", and finally: "pray without ceasing" (1 Thessalonians 5: 17). As a Christian, we need focus on these three elements constantly and consistently to grow in the faith as we approach "the time". Life's pressures and experiences will distract and explode, but we have been "given" the Holy Spirit to infuse and employ.

You can now see the Big 3! If you have read this "Brief", it is likely that you have been given the ultimate opportunity. Do not waste your gift! Exercise the third Trinity and better understand the first and second. Get to work fellow Christian:

The Pay is Unbelievable!

The Messages Of The Scripture #70

On the title page of the 2021 "Briefs", three categories were listed as the unfolding teachings of the "1 Page Briefs". The categories were: Examples, Applications, and Planning. We will unpack those concepts.

1) Examples:

There is nothing more evident in the Bible, then that nothing is new today. Nothing that happens to us is without its past form in history. Human examples include the Patriarchs exemplified by Abraham, Isaac, or Jacob. Passing on, we read of Joseph, Moses, David, Solomon, Daniel, and Jonah to name a few of the more prominent.

Further, we transition from John, the Baptist, through the disciples and the Apostle Paul. As we read through the various lives, I read in wonderment that we have not learned from their mistakes, and improved on this program of life. We are left with the reality of the veracity of Ecclesiastes, and can only agree with Solomon that life is truly meaningless without the inclusion of our Creator and sustainer.

2) Applications:

The myriad examples of Scriptural, Godly, Loving application, are also given to us. How about a pattern for living with others for social-love and caring such as the Ten Commandments (Exodus 20)? How about the extensive guidelines as detailed in the Book of Proverbs? How about the Christ-shared guidelines for loving, caring, and serving, so well noted in the Gospels? One who professes the Christian faith is humbled, or should be, by our Savior's exhortations.

3) Planning For The Future:

It has been researched that almost thirty percent of the Bible is prophetic. This comes as no surprise to me as it was "breathed" by the

Creator, unbridled by time and space. He began with the very first verse stating, "In the beginning". He ended it all in the last days (2 Peter 3: 10), where we are instructed "the heavens will disappear…the elements will be destroyed…the earth will be laid bare". God created everything, sustains everything, and has a perfect plan for our/the future including the earth's planned destruction. "Then I saw a new heaven and a new earth" (Revelation 21: 1). "Behold, I am coming soon" (Revelation 22: 7).

That my friend, sums it up. Take your time: read it, share it, be taught it, and give it away. I have been doing that for at least fifty years. I have no motivation beyond that now in this Godless and sad culture. I now know and appreciate why Christ only hung around for thirty years. I can now understand Noah's flood. I better appreciate the Babylonian captivity. Lastly, I see, but hope not to see, the last seven years of Daniel's prophecy in the book of Revelation.

Get on the good team with me my friend. Not based on your goodness, but based on His goodness. There is punishment, and there is a Hell, but thanks be to God, there is a Heaven.

Please join me on that heavenly trip ☺

The Miracle (?) Of Israel #71

I receive a semi-weekly email from the organ "Prophecy News". This communication keeps me focused on the Middle East where the appearance of a developing Armageddon is playing out. If you have perused the last third of Ezekiel, then you see the end times (latter days) pictured as to the return of the Jewish people to Israel, and all that accompanies that development. If you study the ninth chapter of Daniel, you read the prospects for "Daniel's people". I love the study of the "end times" because we are in them!

A recent rendition focused on the witness of an Israeli resident from the perspective of the Jews who live there today and what they believe. It proves the Godless mentality at present and their ignorance of the Scriptures and prophecy. The Jewish leaders for the most part, lean on the "Talmud" and not the Old Testament.

This particular Jewish immigrant had great pride in the "return" to Israel, but did not recognize God's role in the process. To this individual, it was an act of the will, motivated by worldly rejection. He mentioned how they fought off the enemies over the years discounting any Godly involvement as 5MM Jews fought off 1.5BB Arabs. He was most proud of the emerging state of Israel, and the action of will that his people garnered.

He then gave thanks to a "Higher Force" which gave the USA the motivation to back Israel. Christians note that a Bible-believing Baptist was President at the time, and that Truman recognized the newly formed State. This modern day Israelite finally credited the peoples "chutzpah", and desire to succeed, for the creation of the state of Israel, without crediting God for any of their success. What is new my friend?

God picked, created, and covenanted with the Jewish people to demonstrate the reaction over Millennia of His created people to their Creator. Noah got drunk! The Hebrews built a calf to worship! David murdered and committed adultery! Daniel's contemporaries were also exiled for not resting their land! The Jewish religious leaders of His day crucified Christ! The self-righteous of Paul's day beat him to a pulp! John was sent to a desolate island to die and the Jewish nation of today is secular.

God is the author and sustainer of fidelity and mercy! In Genesis 15, He performs a one way covenant. He puts Abraham into a deep sleep, and covenants to bless him and his children. He also promises them all the land from Egypt to the Euphrates. Now that is something for which to look forward! God made the plan; and He is sticking to it. It has not happened in total yet, but it will. Hundred years ago, we could have still argued about the times, the countries, and the people. But what we have seen in my life, leads one to consider all the prophecies concerning the Jewish people, and God's promised covenant with them.

Are you paying attention my fellow Christian? Have you studied prophetic Scriptures? As Pastor Darrel states, "the world is not falling apart, it is coming together". Are you paying attention? Are you ready?

 It Truly Is: A Miracle

A whole bunch of them! ☺

The Ten Commandments Value #72

I was sharing with a good friend the other day and this topic arose. Is this just a religious issue, for obedience and salvation, or is this a societal set of values? What happens when society takes a dive from sense to nonsense? Have you read about Germany, Russia, or China during the last century? What happens when you throw out the rules for goodness? Some humans just appear to be "evil", and must be controlled. Without those controls society is literally "out of control".

In Godless societies, oligarchs and dictators take over. In these nations military leaders assume power, like Cuba. You have to control the unruly, as they will spew their selfishness on others. There is neither love nor concern except for individual gratification. Standards of living are lowered (note freeway exits and downtown streets in California). Filth is not only allowed, it becomes pandemic. Robberies (smash and grab) and murder grow exponentially. So what's the answer?

The Ten Commandments

Read them lately? Studied them lately? They are in Exodus 20. It begins with "I am the Lord your God"! The first rule excludes all other gods like Buddha, Hindu gods, Allah, or any other substitutes. The second banishes idols. The third says, to not cuss God's name. In America, that is become a pastime of insulting. Now we get into some practical get-along for our everyday lives. Fourth, take a break from your work each week. Fifth, Honor your father and mother? That is gone to hell in a hand basket in America today. Sixth, do not murder. Christ said not to even think about it as in hating or condemning someone (Matthew 5). Seventh, do not commit adultery (or think about it). That is enough said about adultery in this day and age! Searched the internet on your PC or Cell phone lately? Eighth: do not steal. Ninth, do not lie. And finally, tenth, do not covet. If you just passed the test on the above, then you lost it on the tenth. Basically do not want other people's things like your neighbor's car, house, or wife, in a weak moment.

Now let's ice the cake. James 2: 10 says that: "For whoever keeps the whole Law and yet just stumbles at one point is guilty of breaking all of it". Are you kidding me? My friend reminded me that people do things constantly without awareness, or even worse, without remorse. It is so sad to see my country deteriorate from a God-Fearing country to a Godless society. Every school, I believe, should read the Ten Commandments to grade-schoolers and high-schoolers. They can reject it, but they must live it.

So there you have it my reader. Become aware, and have remorse. These are the Creator's rules, both individual and societal. I have seen them thrown out, in my lifetime. It is not working out very well, or at all if you will. Is it too late to turn around? The ancient city of Nineveh did after Jonah's visit. Sodom and Gomorrah did not. You might compare the results. At this late age, I am not too worried;

But my kids should!

Join the faith team! Hang these rules up in your locker. The best is yet to come ☺

The Trinity #73

One of the most mind-boggling exposures to our Creator/God is this concept of the Trinity. This is not my first pass on the topic, but I was impressed by a teaching by Pastor Chuck last week at the start of the Book of Mark, in the Gospels. It had to do with Jesus baptism around His thirtieth birthday. My grandchildren have yet to be baptized in their early 20's, and my son waited until He was fifty, so it was not a hill to die on. In Peter's famous Pentecost prayer (Acts 2: 38), He did say: "Repent… And Be Baptized".

Back to the Trinity! In Genesis 1: 1, the word for God in the Hebrew is Elohim. Now I am no language scholar, but I have been taught, and looked it up in a concordance, and that word is plural. Interesting! In Ephesians 4: 5 Paul writes that there is "one Lord". I could list a whole bunch of "one's" in reference to the God of the Bible, just check your own concordance. This is called understanding the inscrutable. ☺

Please note that Genesis 1 does not exclaim that in the beginning the God created anything, as ancient Greek scholars have written. But there is something relatively inscrutable concerning what the Bible has to say about God. I cannot believe how the Jewish Rabbis and Hebrew scholars missed this particular conjugation and interpretation. They may have been spending too much time focused on Jesus Christ not being their Messiah!

So now to the easier way of seeing it as Pastor Chuck explained. If you turn to Mark 1: 9, then you can read the account of Jesus baptism. Any created human can deal with God, the Father. He is out there somewhere involved or unattached, maybe in creation, maybe not. You need someone to pray to when you are not googling for answers. He can be there first, or existential. Take your pick. If you are a Christian you, then of course believe in God the Son. But what does one do with God the Holy Spirit.

All Christians believe in the Holy Spirit, but the Bible compares Him to the wind. You cannot see Him, but you can "feel" Him when He is moving. You get the picture! But at the baptism, He springs into action. John 3 takes note that John the Baptist "saw" the Holy Spirit descending as a dove. He saw Him, and it was recorded by the author of the Book of John. How did Mark then record the whole event?

Read Mark 1: 9-11(will not take you a minute). Jesus was in the water, He came up, the Father "spoke from Heaven", the heavens opened, and the Holy Spirit "descended" like a dove. Do you get it? God in three persons blessed Trinity!

Maybe you just do not get it. But the Bible says it. It is critical to our faith believing in God the Son. And now, you can see where it comes from. It is just another tidbit/major bit, in the learning process. I really enjoy passing through those levels of learning. Please come along for the ride/education.

It Is A Great Trip ☺

The World, The Flesh, and the Devil #74

That is the battleground folks. My friend Chris led us to James 4: 1-10 at our men's fellowship this morning. It is encouraging to see around two hundred men up at 7AM to study and share the Scripture. James starts out by asking "what causes fights and quarrels?" He answers, that it comes from troubles you have within. "You want something, but do not get it" (verse 2). Does that sound like a day at the office, or a day at home☹? In versa 6 we read: "God opposes the proud, but gives grace to the humble".

But then he continues by addressing the world system within which we live. "Do not you know that friendship with the world (system) is hatred toward God? Hatred? Wow? Now admittedly, James (and the Holy Spirit) is speaking to born-again believers here. This system of accumulating all you can before you die has not worked in the eternal vista, because you leave it all behind. Solomon loved what David left him, but he turned around and left it to his kids. Belshazzar loved all the toys King Nebuchadnezzar left him until the night they partied on with the Jewish utensils, and he saw the handwriting on the wall (Daniel 5).

Lastly we get referenced to the devil. I believe at this late stage, I find him headquartered, or at least vacationing in Vegas; maybe Monaco. Be careful here as the Scripture reads "Submit yourselves then, to God, resist the devil, and he will flee from you" (verse 7). Some folks reverse that order and resist the devil without submitting to God. Be careful, seven sons of a Priest in Acts 19: 14-16, went around driving out demons until one demon asked that they identify. They claimed to act in the name of Jesus until the demon said "I know Jesus and Paul but who are you?" The demon-possessed man proceeded to beat the crap out of them and drive them out naked. "Whoops".

So there you have it, dear reader. As Chris shared you have the problem: internal, the cause: worldly affection and the solution: God's Grace. It was the challenge as a teenager, and I am still battling. As I said to Jason's sons at the table share time, you are thinking in years as you look ahead. I am looking at decades as I reminisce. Just fight the challenge/battle as I did, but include God in your program as the co-pilot.

I hope you are as satisfied as I have been!

Theology The Antichrist #75

Way back in the Old Testament book of Daniel, we learn about the "Abomination of Desolation" referred to by Jesus Christ in Matthew 24: 15. The Book of Daniel was written between 600 B.C. and 550 B.C., by the Prophet himself who was an awesome believer and manager in the empires of exile. This book detailed the future two thousand and five hundred years covering the empires to come and the end of times as we know them. It covered the death of Christ, and the final period of Tribulation.

We will see that not only is this antichrist a personage then, but also people and groups who do what they can to confront the second person in the Trinity, as to His power and divinity. The "antichrist" shows up at the time of "Great Tribulation". In this final period of God's judgment, many believe the third Temple will be constructed, as described in Ezekiel 40. This person will exalt himself and take a seat in the temple as described in 2 Thessalonians 2, "displaying himself as being God".

There is a period when God turns the world and its system over to mankind. This period is called the Tribulation. The activities of this coming period will be activated, motivated, and managed by this individual, worldwide. Daniel spoke accurately in his time, of the coming empires which ruled the expansive Middle East. This ruler will have power over the globe in his time, and gain such influence that he will take a seat in the Temple that is constructed for a three and a half year period. That is when God will bring down the hammer of judgment.

It is all prophesied and will happen!

One common attribute of false theologies today, is an attack of the Jesus Christ of the Bible. He is not God, He is Satan's spirit brother, He is Mohammad's assistant prophet, He did not arise from the dead, He was created, just to name a very few. The Bible shows Jesus as the

Creator, member of the Trinity, sustainer of life, and our ultimate judge. Please look for the "Briefs" as focused.

A lot has happened in my lifetime that would lead thoughts to deduce that we are in the last days of this earthly sojourn. Israel is a country now. Technology allows for digital currency allowing one's ability to buy and sell being controlled. Governments are being forced to consider world global enforcement of rules, and the news is replete with rumors of wars! So open your eyes! See any personalities arising? While there is still time:

Turn To Jesus

He Wins In The End ☺

Theology Who Is God? #76

You would think that to be an easy and answerable question. For almost twenty percent of mankind today, it is answered in the Holy Bible; the bestselling book in the history of mankind. But for close to eighty percent of mankind, all kinds of creative thoughts go toward some kind of answer from Allah, to Krishna, to the evolved Mormon Father, and Baal of the past.

The Bible is explicit and gives multiple verses and paragraphs. I find it interesting that it is the lead verse of the entire text. It is direct, simple, and detailed in the first three chapters. Genesis 1: 1: "In the beginning, God created the heavens and the earth". "So God created man in His own image, male and female, He created them" (verse 27). For a believing Christian, that is perfectly to the point. So what went wrong?

Isaiah 42: 5 renders it: "Thus says God the Lord, who created the heavens and stretched them out. Who spread out the earth, and what comes from it. Who gives breath to the people on it!" (verse 6) I am the Lord; I have called you in righteousness. I will take you by the hand and keep you". How about our personal creation? Jeremiah 1: 5: "Before I formed you in the womb I knew you". Get the point about who God is?

Have you ever wondered about God's personality? He shared that with Moses. Moses had just come down the mountain after receiving the Ten Commandments from God. The stupid Israelites, led by his brother, had melted their gold and created a calf image to worship. He smashed the tablets and later God asked him to create two more for God to etch again. At that point God revealed His personality: "The Lord, a God merciful and gracious, slow to anger, and abounding in steadfast love and faithfulness, keeping steadfast love for thousands, forgiving inequity, and transgression and sin, but who will by no means clear the guilty, visiting the inequity of the fathers on the children, and the children's children, to the third and the fourth generation".

Moses was humbled by that statement, bowed to the earth, and prayed for the forgiveness of his people. He had previously gone forty days without food or drink, in God's presence. He has passed through the Red sea with three million Jews on the way out of Egypt. He had seen the angel of death pass over Egypt selectively, as he saved the young Jewish boys from God's curse of the firstborn. He had started his ministry at the "ripe" old age of eighty years. Hey, this is getting better and better. I think I will write another brief. ☺

So who is God? He is the Creator of everything. Even you! Be thankful you now know this. Be grateful that you know this. God is our Creator and sustainer. You can:

Bet Your Eternal Life!

Theology Denominations #77

Did you ever wonder why we have denominations in the Christian faith? It is rather like the five blind men, each touching a different part of an elephant and asked to describe the animal. One suggests it to be a long tube as he holds the trunk. One describes it as a very large animal as he touches the belly. One describes it as a tiny little growth as he holds on to the tail, and so on.

Have you tried to describe God lately? Have you asked a five year old to define God? Have you asked a middle-aged new convert? Have you asked a seminary graduate? I think you get my point. Yes, there are levels of knowledge, education, and experience, which can unite us or divide us. The burly, hard-bodied fishermen who followed Jesus around (His disciples) tried to shoo away children who were escorted to Christ for a blessing.

Christ rebuked the disciples and said "Let the little children come to me… for the Kingdom of Heaven belongs to such as these" (Matthew 19: 13, 14). Enough Said! On the other hand, Jesus picked a very educated man named Saul, to author half the New Testament as Paul, and please consider his pedigree (Philippians 3). As to the righteousness which is in the Law, found blameless (verse 6). He was trained to be a Pharisee. So you have children versus totally educated. In Jesus' view; who wins?

We have found, over the years, that advanced education is important. It takes great skill and reactive timing to drive a train. But it is meaningless if no one creates and builds it. It takes skill and precision to operate a truck or heavily loaded vehicle, but someone needed to invent it, improve it, and perfect it from steering wheel to foot peddle, to driveshaft, to the breaks.

When someone is "saved", it takes time, experience, and effort to grow in God's Love. Too many attempt to come to conclusive positions too early in the experience. The Corinthian church was like that and especially at communion, when half of them got drunk. 1

Corinthians 13 covers it well. Right at the end of Paul's explanation of God's Love, he describes the obvious process of growing up. Do you know anyone who grew "older" but did not ever grow up? I think you get it!

So cut some slack on fellow believers. Part of growing up is beginning at the Gospel. Then you focus on the teaching and expunge the stuff that takes a great principle too far. Stick with Jesus! Read what He says about Himself, and what Paul says about Him. Do not listen to teachers from the Mormons, J.W.'s, or Muslims. There are some phonies out there, and when you are in grade school, they will confuse you. Even teachers at the college level have various "opinions".

Read Philippians 1: 18, and learn and share the Gospel. Paul said that is what it is all about. Stick with the basics, and do not worry about how educated and sophisticated you attain to if our Lord said Heaven is belongs to the kids. And remember, as I do, that:

Recess Always Came With Kindergarten ☺

Theology: Is Atheism Dying? #78

What a great weekend. I spent most of it listening to one Erik Metaxas concerning his new book entitled "Is Atheism Dead"? This book focuses on the re-emergence of science as a division of the Christian faith. Since the 60's, of the twentieth century, the emergence of modern science has been used, to gradually find a way to mollify the Biblical proofs of a God created existence. To this day in the twenty first century, the effect on many in society seems to be the opposite.

It seems that science, knowledge, computer science, and physics, have gradually developed to the point that the whole universe demands a fine tuning in order to maintain our earthly existence as well as space exploration. We have a family friend who managed the computer department at Jet Propulsion Labs in Pasadena, California. They set up the programs to create rocket ship trajectories or they would not have gotten off the ground to Mars. In anything other than a perfectly created universe, they never would have left this earth!

The interesting spin-off of this whole transition is the conversion of God-damming humans to God-Fearing/blessing personalities. Most notable are the likes of Camus, Sartre, and Flew. A major part of their conversion appears to be just that "fine-tuned" universe. An intelligent human has a hard time believing modern science and the knowledge of the universe to have happened by accident in its beginnings and development over the years.

It would seem than that if one simply believes the Bible as dictated, and then the sciences expounded, the trip would be much quicker, and pre-proven. An why not? The Creator created the Scripture, did not He? Did Erik at this time, create this book commenting on scientific proofs, or did the pages just form one day and the print evolve into lines of words? Get It? Hearing this presented over the weekend was a blessing and an eye-opener. We may soon believe it all began six thousand years ago with thousand sevens left to go for the perfect seven thousand. Know what I am saying?

Genesis 1: 1: "In the beginning, the Triune God created the heavens and the earth"!

Psalm 121: 2 124: 8 "He created Heaven and earth".

Psalm 139: 16: "Your eyes have seen my unformed substance; and in the book they were all written, the days were all ordained for me, when as yet there was not one of them".

Start with the Bible; And Science (and the universe) Will Follow! ☺

Christ Is Preached #79

As I have observed in my lifetime, Christ has been preached various and sundry ways from the pulpit to the television set. Baptism has been marketed from sprinkling to total immersion. Christ is the God of creation to a created emanation from the Spirit world. God speaks to some directly, but to all through His Word. The cross is just that, or it represents a tree. Salvation is through grace or one has to work for it: confused???

A lot of people are, in a world where roughly eighty percent of the population does not know God the Father or His son Jesus the Christ, or for that matter, the Holy Spirit. Given all this confusion, the Apostle Paul straightens the curves with Philippians 1: 18: "What then? Only that in every way, whether in pretense or in truth, Christ Is Proclaimed, and in this I rejoice, yes, and I will rejoice". What has changed? Believe my way! Send me your money. They cannot be Christians when they push that stuff!

For Paul, he wanted the Gospel (Good News) shared (1 Corinthians 15: 3, 4), "For I delivered to you as of first importance, what I also received, that Christ died for our sins, according to the Scriptures, and that He was buried, and that He was raised on the third day according to the Scriptures". Paul continues that Christ was seen by over five hundred people, and that is enough witnesses for me, as well as for Paul himself.

So we have that same situation today, I guess. We have lesser educated people all over T.V. teaching us what the Bible means. We have seminary trained theologians expounding through commentaries and well written exposes'. We have well-meaning individuals like me, sharing thoughts, opinions, and encouragements, without any degreed status. The key for Paul: Get the Gospel preached.

We have just come through a worldwide pandemic of sorts. We are presently witnessing an evil dictator driving into a free country to murder and loot as Stalin or Hitler tried eighty years ago. There is plenty out there to consolidate believers against the evil rulers close to home. We also have faced in recent years; abortion, evolution, sexual immorality, and Godless government leaders. There are numerous antichrist people out there to consolidate our resolve in our faith and forgiveness.

I see this as a continuing buildup in my lifetime which came from our focus on in-fighting. Our culture has changed from a Ten Commandment focus, where we argued with fellow believers in the Gospel, to where we now collectively need face the onslaught of non-belief. We now, must need ask, am I prepared? Have we trained for this? Have I sharpened my Sword?

Preach The Gospel! It Will Soon Be All You Have!

Theology Who Is God #2 #80

In John 1: 1, we start out in the New Testament with another 1: 1. "In the beginning was the Word (Logos), and the Word was with God, and the Word was God". We start out again with another "In the beginning". However, in this rendition, it continues in verse 14 with, "and the Word became flesh". This is self-explanatory to billions, but there are a few million in cults attempting to confuse the obvious. They attempt to destroy Jesus' God-ness, but for the Holy Spirit baptized-saved-individuals it will not work.

If we move to Jesus baptism, then the Spirit of God is brought into the picture. Mark 1: 10,11: "and immediately coming up out of the water, 'He' saw the heavens opening, and the 'Spirit' like a dove descending upon 'Him'; and a voice came out of the heavens, 'Thou' art my beloved 'son' , in 'Thee' 'I' am well-pleased. Do you see it?" The entire "team" comes together for the ceremony: the Father, the Son, and the Holy Spirit.

The purist definition of God for me is "God is Spirit" John 4: 24, and "God is Love" (1 John 4: 8). He then manifests Himself in three ways as the Father. Matthew 6: 9: "Our Father, who art in Heaven; the Son", (Jesus) was calling God His own Father, making Himself equal with God. John 5: 18, and "Peter said…lied to the Holy Spirit…You have not lied to men, but to God" (Acts 5: 3, 4).

What is our job then? Once believing, our job is to work out the salvation we have been given. Jesus defined it aptly on works. "This is the work of God that you believe in 'Whom' He has sent!" (John 6: 29). "This is pure and undefiled religion in the sight of our God and father, to visit orphans and widows in their distress, and to keep one unstained (polluted) by the world (system)" (James 1: 27).

Who is God? The Father, Son, and Holy Spirit! That is what the Bible says. It has taken years to study that out, but the above verses proclaim it. We are talking about the Creator of the Universe, the Creator of life, and the Creator of me. He is more than mankind, He is more than a mover of mountains, or a rocket to Mars. He fine-tuned the Universe, and earth-centered His focus, so I could eventually worship and praise Him eternally.

I sincerely hope all of my family and friends will come around to realize the God of Creation and be blessed as I have and will be!

Transforming And Metamorphosis #81

These words are similar, and yet remind us that in getting right with our Creator makes a difference in one's life, or if you will, makes one a different person. That is the action that emanates from the act. What is the act? Admitting sin and accepting Christ. In that stated act, the action begins. Romans 12: 1, 2 states: "this is your Spiritual act of worship. Do not conform any longer to the pattern of this world, but be transformed by the renewing of your mind".

In a "Brief" in my first volume, I used the illustration of metamorphosis which is the very obvious transformation of a gooey, slimy, caterpillar into a beautiful fluttering butterfly floating through the air. It is quite an amazing "transformation" and used as the same act of salvation and growth in the life of a Christian believer.

In 2 Corinthians 3: 18 we read: "And we who with unveiled faces all reflect the Lord's glory are being transformed into His likeness, with ever-increasing glory which comes from the Lord, who is the Spirit". Did you get that? He just called the Lord, The Holy Spirit. I got it. When Moses spoke with God it was noted that his face became radiant. Exodus 34: 29. We are not only encouraged to this radiance, but spoken of by Paul to have received it.

I picture this life as one of transformation for the believer. Picture people, in general as a gaggle of crawling ugly (?) caterpillars, making their helpless meanderings over the present leaves or bushes to which they have been sequestered. If they eat themselves to maturity, and are not gobbled up by the fortunate local aviator flying in, then they can proceed to the cocoon-ish state and begin the process of transformation. They have been saved.

That begins the cocoon stage which is much like us passing through this life toward glory. Paul says to not be conformed to this worldly process. If I have learned nothing else in this existence, then it is the meaninglessness of this life for me without the active involvement of my Creator; God the father, God the son, and God the Holy Spirit. Someday I will work my way out of this cocoon, they call life. I will flutter away to the beauty of heavenly existence. "I Cannot Wait".

But in the meantime, I will work my way out. Philippians 2: 12: "work out your salvation with fear and trembling". When I emerge from this struggle, it will be beautiful. Do not cut this swaddling cloth from its wrap around my torso. Rather, give me the time and strength to emerge with God's grace and assistance. Unlike the butterfly, I know my destiny. Like the butterfly, I will fly away to glory.

Trust #82

A little over fifty years ago, my wife was with the kids in a local park sandbox. She was reading her Bible and approached by a lady who invited her to a local church. We had just moved to the Santa Clarita Valley, two valleys North of Los Angeles. We gave it a try and found a small but growing fellowship with young couples, and boatloads of children. We fit right in!

They were starting a new Sunday school class/fellowship for couples taught by a man named Terry, and his wife Joy. The study involved a book called "Body Life" and it was a teaching/commentary on the Book of Ephesians. We got involved heavily, and a couple of years later I was teaching the class which had grown to two hundred as Terry moved on to other enjoyments. One thing he did in the process was to have us memorize verses from time to time.

"Trust in the Lord with all your heart, and do not lean on your own understanding. In all your ways acknowledge Him, and He will direct your paths" (Proverbs 3: 5, 6).

I have never forgotten that verse and used it many times over the following decades. While I was growing spiritually during that period, I was losing a business, and can say that the following decade continued as a business disaster for me. But all that time, I continued to trust. I continued to study, and teach (the best way to learn), enjoyed great fellowship, and attended some excellent teaching churches. As I enter my ninth decade now, I look back at having enjoyed a blessed trip, even though I felt at times I was a co-passenger on Paul's boat cruising the Mediterranean Sea.

How does one learn trust (in God)? It is not by being successful! No, you have to go through a process. How does one make wood smooth to finish? They use sandpaper! How does one strengthen their muscles for athletic endeavors? They lift weights until it hurts? How does one increase the flowering buds on a bush or tree? They prune (cut it back) it each year!

163

Look! I am not trying to have you comprehend the process, but it is a process, and that is how it works. You have heard or known spoiled kids, raised in plenty, and never struggling. It is tough to overcome pleasure as opposed to poverty. How many stories do you hear of successful people who were raised in an environment of poverty? As the process unfolds, one can learn to trust in their Creator.

So give it a try. Trust in God! Make friends who also trust in God! You will grow in "wisdom, and stature, and favor with God and men", just like Jesus did (Luke 2: 52). There is also a fantastic reward available at the end of this sojourn; the Millennium, and Heaven! (Revelation 20-22). Enjoy the trip, and make some friends like Terry and Joy. We did!

Trust In The Lord!

Try The Other Side #83

I remember the gas shortages back in the late 70's. Cars would line up for a block to get their tanks filled. The secret was that if you came in from the other direction, then you drove right up to the pump and filled up. Many a time in the early AM or around lunch, I have just parked my car at McDonalds and walked in, ordered at the touch screen, and I am out in minutes. Sometimes it does not pay to "go with the flow" in the drive through line.

Christ applied this action after His resurrection. Just before the cross, He had instructed the disciples to meet Him at Galilee. At the same time He quoted Zachariah 13 where it says: "I will strike the shepherd, and the sheep of the flock will be scattered" (Matthew 26: 31). Do you get this? He told them He was coming back in 3 days, and they still ran and hid. They just did not believe Him.

So these experienced, lifelong fishermen, had returned to their trade of life, and fished the entire night netting the cool waters of the evening, but caught nothing. They knew how to fish, where to fish on that sea, and when to fish. But they came up empty. Christ appeared on shore, and instructed them to cast their nets on the other side of the boat. The nets almost tore apart. There were over one hundred and fifty fish that they pulled in. That was enough to swamp the boat.

They realized it was the resurrected Christ who yelled out the instruction and then headed for shore, fish and all. Peter could not wait, tore off his tunic, and swam ahead. These experienced, well-trained, mature fishermen could not pop a minnow all night, no matter how long or hard they tried. But with one small change in instruction, they hit the jackpot.

Are you really looking for God's intervention and a net full of success? Are you still utilizing hand-me-down programs and techniques to share the Word and God's Love? The world has changed. The culture has changed dramatically in my lifetime. College students today believe in Big Bang evolution as opposed to

165

Godly creation. They have been taught to allow murderers and rapists to live on, but it is okay to murder the unborn. Think about it! What is your approach in this age of non-reason?

Maybe it is time to toss the nets to the other side. I spent a career of successful Regional, and National sales; a product evangelist. I cast the net on the other side multiple times, and it proved very successful. I attend a church across the street from a major University. The church has a couple hundred attendees, and the school has fifty thousand student fish swimming around.

The church ministers are great, and the student ministries are also. I am just wondering if something different could be done by these learned, dedicated, trained, hardworking individuals to fill the nets. You know: standing room only! The preacher happens to be relevant and worth listening to! Good "meat on the bone" stuff for college students in search mode. I might add, the material used is from the bestselling book in human history! It is definitely worth a toss!

Could we toss the nets on the other side? ☺!

Turn Your Radio On #84

In 1972, Ray Stevens sang this song. It is still relevant today as it was in the Billy Graham era of evangelism. The message was simple and to the point, "get in touch with God, turn your radio on". Continuing lyrics say: "everybody has a radio receiver" denoting the principle that each of us is programmed for potential. But as John 1: 12 states, "But as many as received Him, to them He gave the right to become children of God". Now we get into the chicken and egg question!

So what does come first, Grace or Faith? My will or His will? The best answer for me then is Ephesians 2: 8, 9: "For by grace you have been saved through faith, and that not of yourselves, it is the gift of God". In another verse, I note that "just as He chose us, in Him, before the foundation of the world", Ephesians 1: 4. Lastly, "There is none righteous, not even one, there is none who understands, there is none who seeks for God" (Romans 3: 10, 11).

My acceptance of this drives me to give and serve. Why? Because I cannot fathom what I have been given. I have studied the Scripture now for over fifty years, and the ending conclusion is that I have been given very much, including salvation, that I do not seek what this world has to offer anymore. I am so focused on the Millennium (Revelation 20 and Isaiah), and heaven (Revelation 4,21, and 22), that a Beverly Hills mansion pales in comparison; a lottery ticket wins me more material junk, and material success is all eventually left behind, with a lot of it going to Washington D.C..

Ray goes on to sing: "All you got to do is listen for the call". Are you listening? Have you listened? Just reading this "Brief" might jog your conscience. Turn up the volume (if your radio is even turned on). Have you ever noticed how outside noise can drown out your ability to hear your radio? Sometimes I cannot hear the TV as my wife makes noise in the kitchen doing dishes. I turn up the volume or put on my earphones to drown out the noisiness and focus my hearing. That is what the world system does. It is making so much noise from politics to prosperity that it will drown out the sound from our Creators radio station.

I close then with the lyric, "Leaning on the truths that never fail". Did you get that? Every generation goes through levels of forgetfulness. The newest generation does not learn from past mistakes. God's Word, the Scripture, the Bible, cuts through all that with an account of the past, present, and future. Without that Creator guidance, we continue to swim in ignorance, and recreate wars, gain and lose prosperity, and change rulers (political leaders) with impunity.

So "Turn your radio on", my reader. "Get in touch with God". You will love the music ☺

Weakness #85

Did you ever feel weak and run down? Have you been sick for days, or months, or years? I have played football in college and I have lived through a stroke. From having been the fastest runner of the linemen, to sitting in a wheelchair to get around, I know both strength and weakness. From coming from the heaven, to living on earth, to the scourges of His contemporaries, and crucifixion, Christ experienced the true gamut.

Paul was a great example of suffering. What did he do? He believed in Christ, salvation, resurrection, and eternal life. If you wish to hear the result of his sharing that faith, read second Corinthians 11: 23-28. He was jailed, beaten, shipwrecked, and snake bit. Through it all he said: "to live is Christ, to die is gain" (Philippians 1: 21). He reminds us in Hebrews 4: 15, "for we do not have a high priest who cannot sympathize with our weaknesses".

The writer of Hebrews encouraged us in 12: 34 when speaking of Old Testament saints: "from weakness were made strong…" So what is your perspective as you read these examples? Are you transporting through a period of weakness? Is your pain and suffering overwhelming? Nothing on earth can totally diminish that experience in the present. This earthly blessing is wrought with negativity, sadness, pain, and suffering. Do we enjoy the times of blessing and keep perspective during all our experiences?

Christ's example should hold us steadfast: "who for the joy set before Him, endured the cross" (Hebrews 12: 2). Remember an earlier "Brief", a beautiful butterfly must emerge from a cocoon. It is the process. Revelation 21, 22 promise us an eternal existence without pain and suffering. But there is a cost investment. The Old Testament examples of suffering with a saved attitude are multiple. Hebrews 11, lists a few. News reports of Christians in third world areas today are incredible as it relates to persecution and torture.

I ascribe to and work toward Romans 15: 1, "Now we who are strong ought to bear the weaknesses of those without strength and not just please ourselves". Do you have a sick or debilitated friend? Do you have old relatives? Do you know someone in prison? Maybe there is someone close to you who could use a helping hand. Ponder, as you look around where God has planted you:

Do Not Just "Please Yourself"! ☹ ☺

Daniel #1 The Players #86

I am embarking on a "Brief" series, referring to a book in the Old Testament named after its author. In my opinion, Daniel is one of three great men in scripture along with Job, and John the Baptist. There are a lot of great guys who were forgiven, transformed, and followed God with faithfulness and loyalty. But these three guys were almost born to be that way. I am sure as kids, they were nerds. But as grown, dedicated, believers, they were special!

Back to the Book of Daniel! The time frame is in the 500-600 BC's. Israel was being carried off to Babylon for seventy years. Do you know why? They did not rest their farmland every seven years as instructed by God. It is detailed in 2 Chronicles 36:20, 21. Over four hundred and ninety years they chose, as an agricultural culture, to not believe and obey the Creator.

Is there anything that you have been ignoring over the past fifty years? ☹ Please read Jeremiah 25! The timeline is repeated in verse 11, including the King they will serve, and then God punishes the Chaldean Kings for doing what they did. Man, when God gets Mad.

Back to the Book of Daniel! There are three "gaves" in this first chapter: "God gave Jehoiakim, king of Judah, into his (Nebuchadnezzar's) hand" (verse 2)". "God gave Daniel, favor and compassion in the sight of the chief of the eunuchs". This demonstrates God's activity in the daily activities of His created, as well as the historical, and the entire creative process.

As verses jump out at you in your study, grasp them close to your heart, brain, and Spirit. You also can cross that line of belief and faith, where you realize that every line of the Bible can be believed and applied to one's thinking, reasoning, and knowledge.

Back to the Book of Daniel! The first book then sets up the "who" of this prophetic writing. It revolves around Daniel, and his three buddies. His three buddies had three Jewish and Chaldean names. Look them up in chapter one.

In verse 17, we read the third "gave": "As for the four youths, God "gave" them learning and skill in all literature and wisdom, and Daniel had understanding in all visions and dreams". These four even told the chief eunuch, what they would eat. No steak and eggs, they were vegetarians! HMMMMMMM!

So the stage is set. The seventy years are rolling, just as prophesized. The players are in place. God is in the punishment program, and yet uses this period of time in captivity to predict the most profound human event in the history of mankind.

Fasten Your Seat Belts!

Daniel #2 #87

The first half and lengthy diatribe of this chapter deals with King Nebuchadnezzar's dream. He has relied for advice from the King's inner circle, a group of men noted as magicians, the conjurers, the sorcerers, and the Chaldeans. Sounds like Washington DC to me. But He would not take their interpretations unless they can also reveal the dream first. If they do not, they were dead meat.

Daniel steps up. He reveals the dream and the interpretation. It is a picture, in general, and in particular, of coming world powers finalizing with Christ (the Rock). Nebuchadnezzar saw a giant statue in the dream, and Daniel said that it represented future kingdoms including Babylon (the golden head), Persia, Greece, and what most agree, to be Rome.

They would all succumb eventually to the "Rock" (verses 44, 45). Read 31-43 for the details of the statue and the kingdoms. In other words, the statue represented the world controlled by man's power, and the Rock represented the world under the power of Jesus Christ. Get it?

Daniel spoke a blessing in verses 20-23. In it, he noted that God picked and dethroned the Kings of all ages. The key in all of this, to me, is this giant statue revealed to King Nebuchadnezzar, was a picture, in detail, of the coming dynasties. They were powerful and valuable in the future, but nothing compared to the Rock of Jesus Christ who would destroy them in the future and rule forever.

Nebuchadnezzar was so impressed that he made Daniel and his three buddies the rulers over the whole Babylonian province. But the King was fickle, as we see in the next chapter.

The other key share for me in this chapter is why Daniel is considered a prophet of God. In verses 19-23, God shares the dream with Daniel on a 75" flat screen TV (actually scripture calls it a night vision). He then praises God and extols Him for His majesty, greatness, and power. He ends in thankfulness.

Ann Graham Lotz has written a nice commentary on, "The Daniel Prayer" later on in chapter 9. We can now look backwards in history and see that Daniel was spot-on in prophetic history.

We can look at the Bible today and see God's outline for the future. Ezekiel speaks of the end of days, when Israel will be scattered and then return. Is that the country of Israel, I see in place since 1948? According to the Revelation, there is a seven year period coming up that was spoken of in Daniel 9; looking ahead. Wow, this is a fascinating exposé. I cannot wait to study the upcoming chapters. It is like a roller coaster ride; if you will.

Fasten Your Seat Belts!

Daniel #3 The Big Roast, Or Not! #88

This chapter depicts the fiery furnace that we have all heard about from the old Sunday school days. You know, that power, praise, and possessions, can go to a man's head? King Nebuchadnezzar was no exception. This king had a statue erected that was made out of gold. It was ninety feet high and nine feet wide! This makes it one-third the size of the statue of Liberty in New York. However, it was molded from gold. I cannot imagine the value?

Now if that was not enough of an ego trip, the King demanded that when the music began playing at any time or anywhere, people were to face the statue and bow down and worship. That was exactly like today in the Middle East. Minarets blast loud music (noise) five times each day, and Muslims are supposed to bow down to Mecca and worship Allah. Needless to say, Daniel and his buddies refused.

The loyalist leaders understandably obeyed the King and squealed on the Jewish non-compliers. The King was not just displeased, he was enraged. Shadrach, Meshach, and Abed-Nego told the King to pound sand, as they would only worship the God of creation, and not Nebuchadnezzar or his phony gods.

The King hated them, and had them thrown into a furnace which was seven times hotter than usual. The guards throwing them in were all burned to death. Wow! (that is hot)

The "Fickle" King then looked in and saw them walking around, with a fourth guy. King Nebuchadnezzar went near the furnace and called them to come out to safety. This was not 2020 folks where we watch science-fiction on TV. This was a major departure from reality.

He proceeded to command the worship of this Jewish God (as he perceived Him), and no one would be allowed to be critical of their God. I guess He added God (the Creator) to his personal list.

175

This book of Daniel is great. The power of God is demonstrated in the daily lives of these brave believers. God gets real personal, as He did at the Red Sea, at Noah's Ark, at Jesus' Baptism, at the Crucifixion, at Paul's conversion, and finally, at His return in the near future. There are many more times, but this one is really dramatic, and especially in a totally Godless society (Kingdom).

At this point, Daniel's buddies were set for life! The king made sure that they were prosperous from that time forward. He was indeed, impressed. Would not you be? So all I can say in this day of Godlessness is to share your faith, share the Gospel, stand firm in your testimony.

Go Get Roasted!

Daniel #4 Nebuchadnezzar Chopped Down And Saved #89

In this concluding chapter of King Nebuchadnezzar's reign, we see God's Grace in action. The Old Testament stories are depicted so that we see nothing new is going on today. This power hungry, vile, human King, who conquered the known world, murdered people, and took pride in his riches, was literally brought to his knees to eat grass, and lose his mind. All the details are written in chapter 4.

Daniel interpreted another of the King's dreams. He did it in humility, as he said: "My Lord, if only the dream applied to those who hate you, and its interpretation to your adversaries" (verse 19). And then he spoke, "it is Heaven that rules" (verse 26). You need to read chapter 4 and see Nebuchadnezzar's acceptance of this, and then he goes to his roof and takes total honor and praise for the Babylonian Empire.

Interpreters go different directions in analyzing this chapter. One assumes that Daniel took notes, as Nebuchadnezzar spoke of his experience. This is no different than seeing Pharaoh quoted, as he tangled with Moses. Another interpreter sees this chapter, as being written by the King. I think that is a stretch, as the King was no prophet.

Also it was noted that the magicians of the day "could not" interpret the dream. God gave the dream, and He could easily blind the eyes of all but Daniel. So I conclude that Daniel did interpret the dream "alone", and he did write down the King's thoughts and expressions.

It was, after all, dictated in form, substance, and detail, by the Holy Spirit;

But not a hill to die on!

God Strikes Him Down!

The dream plays itself out as the King eats grass, is cursed, and made helpless for seven periods of time. Scripture pictures it as God chopping a tree down to a stump. Not sure by scripture if that is days, weeks, or "years". At any rate, when healed, the King blessed the God of creation in verse 34. He learned by verse 37 that: "He is able to humble those who walk in pride". The Holy Spirit said that he would be protected with an iron or bronze fence until he was brought back to sanity.

Could you use a humbling? Twenty five thousand people in this world die of starvation "each day", and I need to lose thirty pounds. Thousands live on the streets today, especially in warm climates, and I work on a new addition to my residence or a second house for the season. What does Nebuchadnezzar's life show us? Much like Solomon, we just do not handle prosperity and power that well, as created beings.

Our culture has become so prideful. It is because we have forgotten our Genesis. We were created and born; out of the dust. We live and we die, through the Grace of God. We need to share that Grace as we prosper in life. There are plenty of neighbors out there that need our love today. Do not be a Nebuchadnezzar and need to be admonished to reach goodness. "Choose for yourselves, today, whom you will serve" (Joshua 24:15).

Do Not Be A Tree Stump!

Daniel #5 #90

I wanted to entitle this "Belshazzar the Pig", but it seemed inappropriate for a Bible commentary, even if true. King Belshazzar is the son/grandson of King Nebuchadnezzar of the first 4 chapters depending on the commentator. It was three decades later, and Nebuchadnezzar's recognition of the Creator God was long forgotten. This thirty plus year old had multiple wives, and concubines, a besieged city, and decided to throw a party for a thousand sycophants.

They were crazy drunk, and he decided to pull out the Jewish Temple artifacts of gold and silver to use for drinking. Be careful boys and girls, you might just make God mad. Been drunk in your life? I have. You get real stupid! Out of nowhere, some spooky hand appeared, and began writing on the plaster wall. Please refer to chapter 5 for the details. King Belshazzar wanted an interpretation, and the sorcerer's were stumped again, all these years later.

The Queen mother appeared, and suggested that he call on Daniel, as his father had (We assume mother as all his "wives" were drunk by now). Daniel proceeded to interpret the word that you can read in the fifth chapter of Daniel. Daniel said, "God has numbered the days of your Kingdom. You have been weighed, and found wanting. Your Kingdom is divided" (Daniel 5: 26-28).

Daniel castigated the smart aleck King for not remembering what his Dad/Grandpa went through and proceeded to say: Your time is up, you are a lightweight, and I am splitting up Babylon to the next Kingdom. Belshazzar was dead that night.

Do we see parallels today? China, Russia, and India alone have nuclear strength with hypersonic rockets our radar cannot detect. We are getting drunk with alcohol and drugs, thirty trillion dollars in debt, and we murder a million unborn babies each year! I find no problem with the King being wiped out. What about us???

Various writers speak of the Euphrates river that ran through the city being dammed up so the Persians marched in on the dry river bed, opened the gates from within, and the party was over.

Constantly in Scripture, we see the ongoing battle between the Godless and the God-fearing. The God-fearing will always win, but you might not care for the process. I will guarantee you that King Belshazzar did not. Again, we see God actually participating in the details of human life. Many believers believe that we are approaching one of those times again. He is always there, but sometimes it is most dramatic. Seventy year old Daniel saw it again, and will in the next chapter with the Lion's den. Whatever the case, God is in the details.

Do Not Be A Lightweight!

Daniel #6 The Lion's Den #91

Any kid/person who has been through Judeo/Christian Sabbath School has heard two stories: David and Goliath, and Daniel and the Lion's Den. This Lion's den is an amazing picture of Gods entering the cosmos, and affecting a believer's lifetime personally and hands on. You can read about Abraham, Jacob, Moses, David, Christ, and the disciples, but there is none more dramatic then God's encounter with Daniel in the Lion's den.

In chapter 6, we again see the current ruler being aggrandized in his own mind by the ruling sycophant leaders of his day. They ask for a thirty day period of worship for the current King Darius, who signs an edict that he is obviously tricked into doing. The satraps (Congress) set up a form that no one would appeal to anyone but the ruler for petitions of Grace, knowing full well that their leader and "Boss", Daniel prayed daily; petitioning the God of Creation.

He signed, Daniel prayed to God, and the punishment was to be thrown into a den full of hungry lions. Have you ever seen a set of Lion's teeth? They rip African buffalo to shreds with those teeth.

Darius knew that Daniel had a spotless record, and could be trusted with anything including the money. When the crooked satraps exposed Daniel, the King was distraught. He knew that he was tricked, but he had to uphold the law of the Medes and Persians. It says that Daniel knew all about the edict and went to pray anyway. Have you read what has happened to churches meeting during the pandemic of recent? While we claim to be a democracy formed with Judeo Christian principles and freedom.

So Daniel was taken to the den that evening, and the King could not sleep! The King came in the morning, called out, and Daniel asked him to open the sealed den and extract him. The King was overjoyed, and commenced to throw the satraps and, their wives and children in the den. They were dead before hitting the bottom. Lookout Washington D.C.!

I might add that, just like his predecessors, Darius made up a poem/dictum to the God of Daniel; the "Living God". He stated: "His dominion shall be to the end, 'he who has saved Daniel'". Again, God has persuaded a King, until the next Kingdom ☺

Those lions were hungry folks. I love the faith of old Daniel who was now over seventy. He retired in luxury!

Eat You Hearts Out; Siegfried And Roy ☺

Daniel #7 Back To The Future #92

So we ended chapter 6 at the beginning of King Darius' reign, around 520 BC. We then jump back to the first year of Belshazzar's term, around thirty years earlier. Daniel has another dream that was mentioned earlier, outlining the overall program for the future of civilization. For the born-again believer, the Old Testament has prophecies throughout, noting details in the future that must/will take place. Chapter 7 screams them out.

The often-quoted verses in Jeremiah 29: 11, 12, spell out the Spirit of prophecy to Israel: "For I know the plans that I have for you, declares the Lord, plans for welfare and not for calamity, to give you a future and a hope. Then you will call on me, and come and pray to me, and I will listen to you!" The plan is summed up in verses 7: 13, 14. "One, like a Son of man, was coming, that all the peoples might serve Him and His Kingdom is one which will not be destroyed".

That, dear reader is like one being told, you will someday be playing in the Super Bowl, and you will win the game. Jesus Christ will be the winning coach, but He will also be the referee. There will be four playoff games on the way to this finale' and all the "teams" will lose, no matter how successful they appear during the game's progress. I will let you study the chapter to observe the play by play. Myriad books have been written as to the details of this chapter, from a now historical viewpoint as well as the prophetic.

So Daniel is now around seventy years old more or less. He has been in Babylon for around fifty years. He witnessed the fiery furnace and his friend's salvation, He has been given the dream and interpretation of same for Nebuchadnezzar, and he will experience his personal salvation from the Lion's den in the future.

All this time, I might add, Daniel is kept on top of the management heap. Every time he interprets the Kings dream, he gets moved up over the local satraps or rulers, if you will.

The end is repeated in verse 25, where a world leader will speak out against heaven for three and a half years. That sounds like something I studied in the Book of Revelation. He was destroyed in verse 26, and the Highest one will take over in verse 27 and rule for an everlasting period.

Verse 28 ends the Revelation! "At this point the revelation ended. As for me, Daniel, my thoughts were greatly alarming me and my face grew pale, but I kept the matter to myself". Daniel gets another vision three years later that is covered in chapter 8. Suffice it to say, God's laying out the plan for the rest of life in advance. It goes to the end of times.

With The Emphasis On "End"

Daniel #8 The Future Foretold #93

This chapter really exemplifies the nature of this Bible, its author, and in particular, this prophet and his writings. The author, God, Inspires the prophet Daniel (2 Timothy 3:16), and he writes what he is told concerning creation, the universe, and all that will happen in the next few years. One cannot just read this like some fairy tale being made up, but see it as a direct communiqué, from our Creator, personally!

Chapter 8 moves forward to describe the next three iterations of world leaders in the Media/Persian, the Greeks, and then the four spin-offs. Lastly, a maniacal leader emerges who desecrates the Temple of Jerusalem, and even mocks God by sacrificing a pig in the Holy of Holies. Life is not a cake walk as you well know. God has allowed ungodly leaders to rule from time to time, over history, as He lifts His hand of Grace, and allows His adversary Satan to take over for a time, or times.

What gets to me is that the God of our created universe has just spelled out the future for the next four to five hundred years in the future. Once one appreciates the veracity of Biblical prophecies, the Bible becomes a miraculous book of revelation. One can believe in the reality of creation, healing, science, salvation, birth, and everlasting life. I call it the process of transitioning from the known to the unknown.

After decades of study, one comes to realize the reality of our Creator, and His miraculous and detailed involvement in our lives. Daniel receives a revelation, at his city, approximately two hundred miles east of Babylon, in Susa, where he is told through Gabriel the angel; God's future blueprint for the world.

Why? I accept that God is just laying down a framework already planned for the future like He said He would earlier (Jeremiah 29: 11). For I know, the plans I have for you, to give you a future and a hope?

There are many prophesies in the Old Testament, many of which have been fulfilled; such as the Kingdoms and events listed in Daniel 8. I am seeing many of the Ezekiel passages fulfilled today, as Israel has become a country for the Jewish people again in 1948.

Do you think a visit from God is a casual thing? Daniel was sick for days. He also did not get it. But we can! We have seen it happen already. We have seen other predictions take place also. A lot of what we refer to as prophecy, we now call history. What is our advantage then? We can search for the unfulfilled prophecies in Scripture and eagerly await. It is a fun exercise, even if it makes you ill.

If we appreciate, however, that our God of creation is still active in the details of our existence. It is a beautiful thing, if we can pray to our God and know He is ever-present, just as we can Google on our cell phones, it is sustaining, comforting, and keeps us expectant as we read about the Millennium, and Heaven, at the end of the Revelation in Scripture, and know what is "planned" for repentant born-again believers in the future.

Thank You Daniel! Thank You God!

Daniel #9 Jesus Is Prophesied To The End #94

For me, this is one of, if not the most, significant prophecies in the Old Testament. Another might be God telling Abraham about the Exodus four hundred years in the future in Genesis 15. Another might be Micah 5, predicting the birthplace of the Messiah. Another, the seventy years of captivity noted in Jeremiah and Daniel. But in Daniel 9: 24-27, we see a dated prediction of four hundred and ninety years of which all but seven are accounted for. This is not just amazing, it is absolutely incredible!

So how did Daniel start this particular vision? He, of course, dated it and identified it as Darius's first year as King over the Babylonians (Chaldeans, 522 B.C.). He quoted Jeremiah who said that the Jewish captivity was for seventy years (Jeremiah 29: 10). And then "I turned my face to the Lord God. I prayed to the Lord my God, and made confession" (verse 3). I am still looking forward to the day that I can say that I prayed and fasted with any regularity. That would put me in the company of Daniel, Moses, David, and Jesus. That is quite a group.

Before the most significant prophecy in history, Daniel went on to confess his sins and pray for the sins of Israel. It was all in the first 19 verses of Chapter 9. Please read the above-mentioned, and see if he was not praying for you and me also! The Angel Gabriel then appeared to Daniel telling him how much Daniel was loved in Heaven, and imparted this detailed vision and time prophecy:

"Seventy weeks (7X70 years = 490 years) are decreed for your people", "to put an end to sin", as judgment is completed and heaven is opened for Christ's saved (that must speak of the end of this world, for sure). It predicts the death of Christ, and leaves one seven year period to be fulfilled. I personally feel that we are approaching that time period in 2022.

I would like that my grandkids could look forward to long lives filled with children, but that does not look probable as Israel has re-formed under Jewish rule, which is what the Bible refers to as the beginning of birth pains. Get the picture???

Verse 25 predicts from the time of King Artaxerxes until the Messiah's death is four hundred and eighty three years; as it was! Jerusalem will be rebuilt and, in verse 26, Jesus will die, and the city will be destroyed by the Romans; and it was! In strange language, it states a desolation will occur with an individual signing a peace pack for the world until three and a half years are over. He then enters the Temple as God, until the true Creator God puts an end to it all and Christ returns (Zachariah 14, Matthew 24, 2 Thessalonians 2:8).

This covers it all folks. It only takes more or less twenty five thousand years. It is capsulated in two verses, but true. Most of it has already happened.

Can You See The Finish Line? Please Get In The Race!

Daniel #10 #95

These visions are coming decades apart, so the chapters of Daniel are not chronological. What we see in chapter 10, is a Damascus road experience. Daniel gets a Word, fasts and prays for three weeks, and then sees a vision of a radiant angel (?). He alone sees the angel but those around him feel a trembling and run to hide. Daniel is on the bank of the Tigress River, so he does get around the kingdom. Last time we heard from him, he was at Susa. Another thing had changed over the years, Daniel was no longer a vegetarian, and he also drank wine.

Daniel felt led to pray, and had heard nothing after three weeks of prayer and fasting. The personality touched him, and Daniel was weakened to falling down. The angel explained that Daniel had been heard at the outset, but it took twenty days for the visitor to get through the battlegrounds fighting the prince of Persia. The angel needed Michael to assist him in his passage. It was the same battle described in Ephesians 6:12 (We do not fight against flesh and blood).

The message conveyed to Daniel was that the angel was off to fight the prince of Persia so that the prince of Greece could take over, just as Daniel had earlier foretold. This angelic visitation was quite debilitating to Daniel. The angel again touched him to strengthen him. I am not sure what the purpose was in this chapter/vision, but I do believe that it was to communicate that a great deal is happening behind the scenes in a Spiritual dimension constantly! It also conveyed that Daniel was "greatly loved" by heaven.

The next chapter takes place fourteen years later. Daniel was apparently a busy guy running the empire(s). Travelling from Babylon to Susa, and back, was no short venue in the day. Daniel was also around seventy years old, which was significant in those days. The angel went off, and joined Michael to introduce the Grecian Empire. I surmise that in the Spirit world, time was not a factor; but I speculate.

189

The main thing to me is the connection between the two worlds (material and Spirit).

I sincerely believe God introduced the Book of Daniel to demonstrate God's power of intervention, and to lay out His plan for the next twenty five thousand years. It seems to be rolling out, according to plan.

Daniel #11 #96

To me personally, Chapter 11 is the most difficult chapter in Daniel to digest. I have attached a couple commentaries to help explain the details. It is basically an overview of the next five hundred years, more or less. It goes into extensive detail with powers from the North and South of Israel fighting each other. It touches on the desecration of the temple and the "abomination of desolation". It mentions attacks coming from the sea as well, this "king" ruling the "beautiful Holy Mountain", and then coming to an end.

The attachments help the picture become understandable, but what we see here is an overview of coming events. Why is that significant, you ask? Because it shows that God has plans down to the details of who is in charge, who will win, and who will lose in the future. At the time of Daniel's vision, it would have been total speculation and confusion. Today it has transpired, been noted historically, and gives us confidence in unfulfilled prophecy in our day. It Will Happen!

As usual, Daniel starts with the date of the vision. It has been over a decade since his last encounter, as Daniel continues in his task of ruling. I look forward to the other side, when I can review the life of Daniel, and see what kept him busy during these decades. He was a prominent ruler who never gave an inch on his faith, and lasted through four different rulers. That was beyond amazing. He must have been a brilliant manager.

What I get out of this period of prophecy and history, is God's disgust with His chosen people and chosen land. Nations war back and forth over the top of Israel, and it ends up in the hands of Herod at the time of Christ. It is my understanding that the priesthood had left the lineage of Zadok, which was a Godly mandate. This is why Christ so hated the Pharisees and Scribes of His day. The Book of Malachi castigates the leadership and unfaithfulness in Israel, and there is a five hundred year period of deadness before the Gospels.

So that is the story! That was the story, and that will be the story. I repeat that I feel, personally, that the purpose of this Book, and in particular, this chapter, is to point out that the artist of creation, our God and Savior, has created and designed, and planned the details of past and future history. I have, am, and will enjoy this trip to the fullest extent. Thank you Daniel for being there! Thank you God for using Daniel to share these messages! I believe that the most fun part, good and bad, is yet to come.

Allllllllll Aboard!

Daniel #12 The End Is Here #97

So, we come to a close for God's prophet Daniel. He was around a hundred years old, and I am not sure if they retired in those years, but his tires were certainly worn bare. He had just heard the bad news from up North and back East. Today that could include Turkey, Russia, Iran, and China. Unstoppable! So God brought Michael back in, who God noted, is the Spiritual angel of the Jewish nation. It noted that this will be the "Time of the End", but Daniel is kept in the dark.

In the next section, we see a time period is laid out: three and a half years! Sound familiar? There are some times set up which do extend this particular holocaust, but it is basically the Great Tribulation. He further states that the wise will understand, and the wicked will act wickedly. I believe what one can see here is the emergence of Israel as a country with which to reckon.

Without the Creator's involvement however, this is absurd. Ask Gideon, the warrior Prophet! We see this prophesied at the end of Amos 9: 11-15. "I will restore the fortunes of my people Israel" (verse 14), "and they shall never again be uprooted" (verse 16).

Jesus covers the picture in Matthew 24, where He explains the details including the anti-Christ in the Temple (third?), and the "Son of Man coming on the clouds". In Ezekiel 47, we see the new topography, as Christ has returned for His thousand year reign. Upon landing the Second Coming on the Mount of Olives, waters emerge and drain to the Mediterranean Ocean, and the Dead Sea. There is so much water spewing from the Temple base that the Dead Sea comes alive, and they catch fish in it.

As Paul and Barnabas came to the disciples in Acts 15, James confirmed to them, "I will rebuild the Tent (third Temple?) of David that has fallen; I will rebuild the ruins" (verse 16). In Revelation 20, we see that the return of Christ, where all who refused the Mark of the Beast reigned with Christ for those thousand years. What a glorious period of time for us believers. I think Isaiah covers the transition well in chapter 66: 15-24. He brings judgment to unbelievers and Grace to believers. The focus will be "my Holy Mountain Jerusalem" (vs 20)

So God does speak with mystery, even to and through His prophets. He wants us to know, obviously, that a plan is in place. Not just a plan in general, but a plan with the specifics in place. I have jumped about, to demonstrate this is more than happenstance. God brings up the future end times that have and will happen. Daniel's visions, prophecies, and experiences paint the picture of past, present, and future. As it has taken place, we see God's involvement, even to Lion's dens and fiery furnaces. Nothing more is necessary to prove the veracity of future predictions.

So God tells Daniel that the final time period will be three and a half years. He tells Daniel that sacrifices will take place until the Abomination of Desolation takes a seat in the new Temple. He tells Daniel, that a few more days will be added. However no one seems to know what is involved in that extra few days. God keeps mysteries. Christ even said: "only the Father knows the day and the hour" (Mark 13:32). God closes His revelation to Daniel: "And you shall rest and you shall stand in your allotted place at: The End Of Days"! It Is Coming Dear Reader!